SASHA KAGAN'S
Country
Inspiration

SASHA KAGAN'S
Country Inspiration

Knitwear for All Seasons

SASHA KAGAN

Photographs by Jack Deutsch

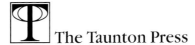
The Taunton Press

Publisher: Jim Childs

Acquisitions Editor: Jolynn Gower

Assistant Editor: Sarah Coe

Copy Editor: Candace B. Levy

Art Director: Paula Schlosser

Cover and Interior Designer: Carol Singer

Layout Artists: Carol Singer and Rosalie Vaccaro

Photographer: Jack Deutsch

Illustrators: Sasha Kagan, Carla Patrick Scott, and Rosalie Vaccaro

Taunton
BOOKS & VIDEOS
for fellow enthusiasts

Printed in the United States of America

10 9 8 7 6 5 4 3 2 1

The Taunton Press, Inc., 63 South Main Street, PO Box 5506,
Newtown, CT 06470-5506

e-mail: tp@taunton.com

Distributed by Publishers Group West

Library of Congress Cataloging-in-Publication Data

Kagan, Sasha.

   Sasha Kagan's country inspiration : knitwear for all seasons / Sasha
Kagan; photographs by Jack Deutsch.

    p.   cm.

    ISBN 1-56158-338-3

   1. Sweaters. 2. Knitting—Patterns. I. Title: Country inspiration.

   II. Title.

TT825.K3284   2000

746.43'20432—dc21   99-052956

For my mother, source of all inspiration

Acknowledgments

First, my sincere thanks to Jeni Morrison, pattern writer, finance manager, and confidante, whose unerring faith in my creativity has brought this book to fruition.

Second, to those who make up my dedicated team: Marlene Richards, for making up and finishing each piece to perfection; Muriel Jones, for knitting the swatches in next to no time and crocheting the trims on the sweaters and soft furnishings; and my knitters, Lilian Bannister, Chris Bebbington, Lily Collison, Muriel Follis, Betty Gwilliams, Pennie Hawkins, Doreen Hill, Bernice Ingram, Marion James, Jean Pashby, Mary Philips, Jenny Remington, Lucy Trembath, Betty Webb, Ruth White, Mary Withington, Barbara Wiltshire, and Pauline Ziontek, for their hand-knitting skills and the long hours spent crafting the pieces.

Third, to Rowan Yarns for letting me play with their extraordinary range of colors, textures, and blends created at their mill in Yorkshire; to their director Stephen Sheard for his support; and to Kathleen, Karen, and Elizabeth for sending me the yarn so promptly.

The Welsh photo shoot was a delightful experience. It was a pleasure to introduce New York photographer Jack Deutsch to my landscape and to work with the models—my daughter, Tanya, and her friend Cori—and stylist and hair and makeup artist Lucy Campbell. Clothes for the shoot were kindly lent by Warehouse (London) and Glenarmon Tweed (Scotland). Shoes were from Faith (London), and tights from Wolford.

A big thank you to Jolynn Gower and Sarah Coe of The Taunton Press for their sensitive presentation of my work.

And finally, to all my fans who knit and wear my designs. Without you I would not have made this collection.

Contents

Roses

Autumn Leaves

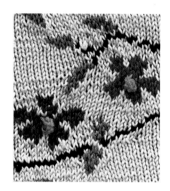

Meadow Flowers

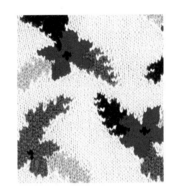

Forest Fruits

Cottage Garden

Techniques

Introduction

Dear Knitters,

The countryside is the inspiration for my third collection of patterns for hand knitting. In this book, I wanted to convey my love of each season: the changes from the brave snowdrops of winter to the delicate wildflowers of spring, from the full-blown roses of summer to the glorious rusts, ochers, coppers, and greens of the leaves of autumn.

For the past 27 years, my home has been the idyllic countryside of mid-Wales. Here the winters are long—so long—and I welcome each sign of spring. Living with the seasons and tending my garden whenever possible makes me tune in to what is happening on the 13 acres of wooded hillside that I care for. This collection is about my life in the Welsh landscape, but I have tried to make it relevant to all those who, like me, love the countryside.

The countryside makes me nostalgic for my childhood spent in Cambridgeshire, where I would wander through the fields collecting wildflowers to press, paint, and draw. There I was encouraged by my mother to use textiles as a medium of expression. She was herself an inspired dress designer, expert crocheter, knitter, and lampshade maker. I seem to have inherited not only her obsession with fabric but her attention to detail. The three-color striped twisted rib used in Rowanberry to accentuate the construction of the jacket, the knitted frill and the invisible pockets used in Cable Rose to complement the intarsia roses and textures of the fabric, the chenille collars of Hawthorn Berries and Dancing Leaves—all these remind me of the beautifully tailored clothes my mother made me when I was a child.

In *Sasha Kagan's Country Inspiration* I have tried to offer hand knitters a large choice of projects both for womenswear and the home. The sweaters use my signature classic shapes; and combined with an exuberant joy in timeless rural imagery, the finished pieces will always stay in fashion. And, of course, knitted soft furnishings give a country feel to any interior. Hand-knitted garments have a warmth and magic entirely absent from machine-made items. They are crafted with love and are often intended as a gift for a loved one. I have some shawls knitted by my mother that are family heirlooms, and I know that many of the pieces in this collection will be knitted with love to become heirlooms in their turn.

I hope you enjoy the designs in this collection. When you knit them yourself you will have helped continue the tradition of hand knitting into the 21st century.

I do not believe that any artist can exist without feedback from the public. I love the dynamism of lecture tours and workshops, and I look forward to meeting some of you there and to discussing hand knitting.

Sasha Kagan

How to Use This Book

YARNS

The major ingredient of a textile is, of course, the yarn. The majority of my designs use the wonderful palette from Rowan Yarns, whose range of color and texture is amazing. I have used paint names as well as Rowan names to describe the colors in case the exact shade numbers become unavailable throughout the life of this book. For Gypsy Rose I chose Colinette yarn, because the voluptuous roses demanded the subtlety of random dip-dyed fibers. The Violets ballet wrap uses Jamiesons & Smith's four-ply Shetland, a yarn that dates to the 1940s. For some of the delicate, floaty Rose designs, I have used my own four-ply wool/silk mixture. And when Jaegar introduced a four-ply cashmere, I could not resist playing with it, the most luxurious of fibers, for the Anemone and Wildflower designs. All yarns are from Rowan; unless otherwise noted (see p. 170 for sources).

The finishing touch to a piece is always the buttons. In this collection, I have used antique buttons from Duttons for Buttons in Harrogate and hand-carved wood and bone buttons made by the Latchmi Sharma Women's cooperative in Nepal.

From experience, I know that some of you may have difficulty obtaining the precise shades of yarns and accessories called for. It may be more convenient for you to buy a complete knitting kit directly from my studio.

My knitters always feel a little sad when a collection is finished: They tell me of small nuances of manufacture that they would like to use when they knit the piece again. So do not feel too guilty about being unable to knit one of the designs yourself: You can order a ready-made piece from my studio team. My knitters like to know the name of the individual who has ordered an item. I think this is because there is a warm bond that extends from the knitter to the wearer. Don't you agree that knitting is about the warmth of a family?

CHARTS

The colored charts in this book provide the information for producing the motifs on each piece. Each square on the chart equals one stitch in a horizontal direction and one row in a vertical direction. The color of the square denotes the color of the yarn to be used, so these can be easily identified as you knit. Stockinette stitch (stocking stitch) is used throughout, except where indicated on the chart. The designs start at stitch 1 on Row 1 at the bottom right-hand corner with a knit row and are read from right to left. After reaching the end of Row 1 on the chart, start again at stitch 1, and repeat the process until you have come to the end of the stitches on your needle. The next row, a purl row, begins directly above the last stitch, and this row is read from left to right.

On reaching the top of the chart, you should return to Row 1 and repeat the process as many times as are necessary for the piece. Sometimes you will be told to return to a particular row when repeating the chart. This is necessary in a design such as Dancing Leaves to link the motifs and in other designs such as Ash that start with a border.

There are other designs for which you will be told to produce a mirror image on the left and right fronts or on the sleeves, and this is done by purling Row 1 from right to left and knitting Row 2 from left to right and continuing in this manner to the top of the chart. For some designs, alternate workings of the chart need to use this device to keep the motifs flowing correctly, for example, Ivy.

Some designs need to have a different placing for the front or sleeves, because the chart used for the back of the garment would not correctly position the motifs on other parts of the garment. In this case, you will be told to start the chart at a different stitch from stitch 1; for example, this is used when placing the motifs on the fronts and sleeves of Leaf Chain.

INTARSIA

All but one piece (Gypsy Rose Coat) in this book use the intarsia method of working the motifs. A separate ball, or length of yarn is used for each separate block of color across the row, so that the yarns are not carried across the entire row. The background yarn is carried across the back of the work, preferably woven across, not stranded.

The exception—Gypsy Rose Coat—is made with individual motifs for which the background yarn is not carried across the back. To avoid gaps when working an individual motif, it is very important to secure the color changeover points. When you move from one color to the next, firmly twist the yarns around each other where they meet on the wrong side.

TERMINOLOGY

The instructions in this book have been written so that both American and British knitters can follow them. In all cases, the American term appears first followed by a slash (/) and then the British term, for example, bind off/cast off.

> **TIP:** To avoid having to roll large numbers of small balls, cut lengths of yarn as required. The first time you work a motif make a note of how many stitches you get to an inch of yarn; then you will be able to cut quite accurate lengths for the rest of the garment.

Kits, including the yarn and buttons (when applicable), to make the pieces in this book are obtainable by mail order from:

Sasha Kagan Knitwear, The Studio, Y Fron, Lawr-y-glyn, Caersws, Powys (Wales) SY17 5RJ UK
(+44) 01686 430436
www.sashakagan.com

ABBREVIATIONS

alt	alternate(ly)
approx	approximate(ly)
beg	begin(ning)
C	cable
C1F	cable 1 front: slip next stitch onto a cable needle and leave at front of work, K2, then K1 from cable needle
C2B	cable 2 back: slip next 2 sts onto a cable needle and leave at back of work, K1, then K2 from cable needle
C4B	cable 4 back: slip next 2 sts onto a cable needle and leave at back of work, K2, then K2 from cable needle
C4F	cable 4 front: slip next 2 sts onto a cable needle and leave at front of work, K2, then K2 from cable needle
C6	cable 3 back: slip next 3 sts onto a cable needle and leave at back of work, K3, then K3 from cable needle
ch	chainstitch
cont	continue(ing)
dc/tr	US double crochet/UK treble crochet
DDK	designer double knitting
dec	decrease(ing)
DK	worsted weight/double knitting
foll	follow(ing)
g	gram(s)
hdc/htr	US half double crochet/UK half treble crochet
inc	increase(ing)
K	knit
m1	make 1 stitch by winding the yarn around the needle and treating this as a stitch on the next row
mm	millimeter(s)
P	purl

patt	pattern, work in pattern
psso	pass slipped stitch over
rem	remain(ing)
rep	repeat(ing)
RS	right side
sc/dc	US single crochet/UK double crochet
sl 1	slip 1 st from the left-hand needle onto the right-hand needle
sl st	slip stitch
st st	stockinette stitch/stocking stitch
st(s)	stitch(es)
tog	together
WS	wrong side
yfwd	yarn forward
yo	wind the yarn over the needle to make a stitch
( )	repeat instructions inside parentheses as many times as instructed

KNITTING NEEDLE AND CROCHET HOOK SIZES

Knitting Needles

Metric	US	UK
2¾ mm	2	12
3¼ mm	3	10
3¾ mm	5	9
4 mm	6	8
4½ mm	7	7

Crochet Hooks

Metric	US	UK
0.75 mm	12 steel	13
1.50 mm	6 steel	12
2.00 mm	B/1	10
3.00 mm	D/3	9
3.50 mm	E/4	8

Roses

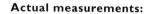

Victorian Rose Peplum

VICTORIAN ROSE

Actual measurements:
bust 33", center back neck to welt 25",
sleeve seam 19½"

Gauge/tension:
26 sts and 32 rows to 4" on
3¼-mm needles over patt

INSTRUCTIONS

SPECIAL INSTRUCTIONS:
BOX PLEAT (WORKED OVER 40 STS)
Row 1 (RS): sl 1 purlwise, K38, sl 1 purlwise.
Row 2: P40.
Rep these two rows 26 more times (54 rows in all).

BACK

With 3¼-mm needles and Garnet cast on 248 sts.
Work chart from bottom to top and Box Pleat for 54
rows and, **at the same time,** dec 1 st at each end of
3rd row and every foll 4th row 8 times as foll:
Row 1: patt 39 sts, make pleat over next 40 sts, patt
next 25 sts , make pleat over next 40 sts, patt next 25
sts, make pleat over next 40 sts, patt rem 39 sts.
Row 2: patt 39 sts, (P40, patt 25 sts) twice, P40, patt
39 sts.
Cont in patt as set to Row 54.
Row 55: patt 24 sts (bind off/cast off next 40 sts, patt
25 sts) twice, bind off/cast off next 40 sts, patt 24 sts
(98 sts).
Row 56: patt across all 98 sts, taking care to pull yarn
tightly as each patt block is brought tog at pleat.
Work a further 4 rows in patt.

MATERIALS

- 25 g Raspberry wool/silk
- 50 g Plum fine cotton chenille
- 50 g Maple fine cotton chenille
- 50 g Pale pink fine cotton chenille
- 2 x 50 g Willow fine cotton chenille
- 50 g Olive wool/silk
- 7 x 50 g Garnet grainy silk
- 1 pair 3¼-mm (US 3, UK 10) needles
- 3.00-mm (US D/3, UK 9) crochet hook
- 1 stitch holder
- 17 buttons

Side shaping: inc 1 st at each end of next and every foll 6th row until there are 120 sts.

Work a further 9 rows.
Armhole shaping: bind off/cast off 6 sts at beg of next 2 rows (108 sts).
Work a further 62 rows in patt.
Shape back neck: patt 46 sts, turn and place rem sts on a stitch holder.
Work each side of neck separately.
Bind off/cast off 7 sts at beg of next row and foll alt row.
Bind off/cast off rem 32 sts.
With RS facing, rejoin yarn to rem sts, bind off/cast off center 16 sts, patt to end.
Work 1 row, then complete second side to match first side, reversing all shapings.

LEFT FRONT

With 3¼-mm needles and Garnet cast on 104 sts.
Then work in patt from chart for Left Front, working Box Pleat as given for Back in position shown on chart and, **at the same time,** dec 1 st at beg of 3rd row and at same edge on every foll 4th row 6 times, then every foll 3rd row 8 times.
Cont in patt as set to Row 54.
Row 55: patt 24 sts, bind off/cast off next 40 sts, patt 25 sts (49 sts).
Row 56: patt across all 49 sts, taking care to pull yarn tightly as each patt block is brought tog at pleat.
Work a further 4 rows in patt.
Side shaping: inc 1 st at beg of next row and at the same edge on every foll 6th row until there are 60 sts.
Work a further 9 rows in patt.
Armhole shaping: bind off/cast off 6 sts at beg of next row, patt to end (54 sts).
Work a further 38 rows in patt.
Front neck shaping: bind off/cast off at beg of next row and foll alt rows: 5 sts once, 4 sts twice, 3 sts once, 2 sts once, and 1 st twice.
Work 3 rows, then dec 1 st at beg of next row and foll 4th row.
Work a further 8 rows.
Bind off/cast off rem 32 sts.

RIGHT FRONT

Work as for Left Front, reversing all shapings and foll chart for Right Front.

SLEEVES

With 3¼-mm needles and Garnet cast on 46 sts.
Then foll chart for Sleeves for 170 rows and, **at the same time,** inc 1 st at both ends of Row 17 and every foll 4th row until there are 112 sts, working extra sts in Garnet only.
Cont straight until work measures 19" from cast-on edge.
Bind off/cast off.

MAKING UP

Tidy loose ends back into their own colors. Pin Box Pleats into position, then sl st carefully into place. Press Box Pleats lightly with a warm iron over a damp cloth. Join shoulder seams. Sew Sleeve into armhole, the straight sides at top of Sleeve to form a neat right angle at bound-off/cast-off sts of armhole at Front and Back. Join rest of Sleeve and side seams.

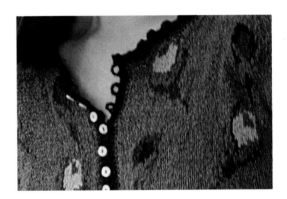

CROCHET EDGING

Round 1: With 3.00-mm crochet hook and Plum and RS facing, work 1 row sc/dc evenly up Right Front edge, round neck edge, down Left Front edge, and across bottom edge of garment, including pleats.
Round 2, Picot Trim: *sl st along 3 sc/dc of previous row, 3 ch, sl st into same place*. Rep from * to * to end. Fasten off.
Work Rounds 1 and 2 of picot edging around cuffs.
Sew buttons to Left Front edge, the first at start of neck shaping and the last at the waistline. Use picot loops to form buttonholes and space accordingly.

Press lightly with a warm iron over a damp cloth.

Victorian Rose Peplum

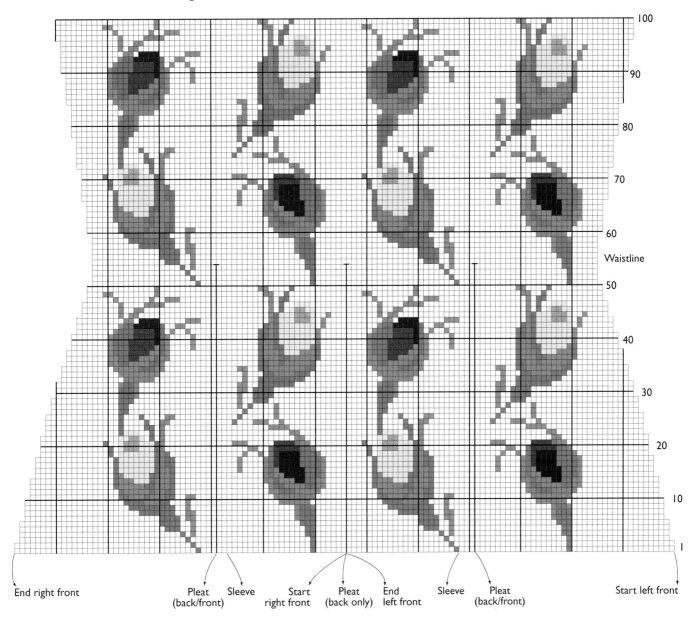

100 — 90 — 80 — 70 — 60 — Waistline — 50 — 40 — 30 — 20 — 10 — 1

End right front | Pleat (back/front) | Sleeve | Start right front | Pleat (back only) | End left front | Sleeve | Pleat (back/front) | Start left front

100-row patt rep. Rep from Row 1.

Color Key

■ Raspberry ■ Willow
■ Plum ■ Olive
■ Maple □ Garnet
□ Pale pink

Victorian Rose Edge-to-Edge Jacket

Actual measurements:
bust 46", center back neck to
welt 20½", sleeve seam 18½"

Gauge/tension:
26 sts and 31 rows to 4" on
3¼-mm needles over patt

INSTRUCTIONS

BACK

With 2¾-mm needles and Apricot cast on 150 sts.
Work 1" st st ending with a P row.
Next row: work a picot edge (yfwd, K2 tog) to end.
Work 3 rows st st.
Change to 3¼-mm needles and work chart from bottom to top once, then from Row 9 until work measures 20" from picot edge line.
Shape shoulders: keeping continuity of patt bind off/cast off 18 sts at beg of next 6 rows. Bind off/cast off remaining 42 sts.

LEFT FRONT

With 2¾-mm needles and Apricot cast on 74 sts.
Work 1" st st ending with a P row.
Next row: work a picot edge as for Back.
Work 3 rows st st.
Change to 3¼-mm needles and work chart from bottom to top once, then from Row 9 until work measures 16" from picot edge line, ending with a K row.
Neck shaping: keeping continuity of patt bind off/cast off 3 sts at beg of next 2 alt rows.
Bind off/cast off 2 sts at beg of next 2 alt rows.
Bind off/cast off 1 st at neck edge on next 10 alt rows (54 sts).

MATERIALS

- 2 x 50 g Catkin fine cotton chenille
- 2 x 50 g Willow fine cotton chenille
- 25 g Pale yellow lightweight DK
- 50 g Mustard wool/silk
- 25 g Peach lightweight DK
- 2 x 50 g Apricot wool/silk
- 6 x 50 g Apple wool/silk
- 1 pair 2¾-mm (US 2, UK 12) needles
- 1 pair 3¼-mm (US 3, UK 10) needles

Cont straight until Front measures same as Back to shoulder, ending with a P row.
Shape shoulder: keeping continuity of patt bind off/cast off 18 sts at beg of next 3 alt rows.

RIGHT FRONT

Work as Left Front, reversing all shapings and beg chart at st 27.

SLEEVES

With 2¾-mm needles and Apricot cast on 50 sts. Work 1" st st ending with a P row.
Next row: Work a picot edge as for Back.
Work 3 rows in st st.
Change to 3¼-mm needles and work chart as for Back, and **at the same time,** inc 1 st at both ends of next and every foll 4th row until there are 116 sts. Cont straight until work measures 18" from picot edge line.
Bind off/cast off.

FRONT BANDS (BOTH ALIKE)

With 3¼-mm needles and Apricot and RS facing, pick up and K 1 st for every row along front edge between picot edge and neck. Then foll chart from Row 1 to Row 8 (border chart).
Change to Apricot and P 1 row.
Next row: work a picot edge as for Back.
Change to 2¾-mm needles and work 1" st st.
Bind off/cast off.

NECKBAND

Join shoulder seams.
With 3¼-mm needles and Apricot and RS facing, pick up and K 1 st for each row from 3 sts after picot edge to 3 sts before picot edge around neck.
Then foll chart from Row 1 to Row 8 (border chart).
Change to Apricot and P 1 row.
Next row: work a picot edge as for Back.
Change to 2¾-mm needles and work 9 rows st st.
Bind off/cast off.

MAKING UP

Tidy loose ends back into their own colors. Position top of Sleeve so that center is at shoulder seam and sew in place. Join Sleeve and side seams. Turn all facings to inside and sew into place. Press lightly with a warm iron over a damp cloth.

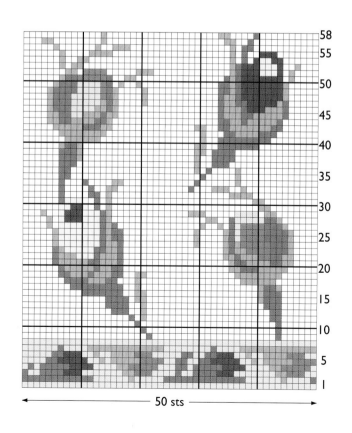

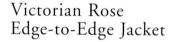

50 sts

Victorian Rose
Edge-to-Edge Jacket

Color Key

Catkin

Willow

Pale yellow

Mustard

Peach

Apricot

Apple

Rose Rib Turtleneck Sweater

Actual measurements:
bust 34", center back neck to
welt 21", sleeve seam 17"

Gauge/tension:
25½ sts and 28 rows to 4" on
4-mm needles over patt

INSTRUCTIONS

BACK
With 4-mm needles and Charcoal cast on 132 sts.
Foll chart from bottom to top until work measures
12½", ending with a P row.
Shape armhole: keeping continuity of patt, bind
off/cast off 6 sts at beg of next 2 rows.
Dec 1 st at both ends of next 8 rows (104 sts)*.
Cont straight until armhole measures 8½", ending
with a P row.
Shape shoulders: keeping continuity of patt bind
off/cast off 8 sts at beg of next 6 rows.
Place rem sts onto a stitch holder.

FRONT
Work as for Back to *.
Cont straight until armhole measures 5½".
Neck shaping: keeping continuity of patt work 44 sts,
turn and place rem sts on a stitch holder.
Work each side of neck separately.
Working on this set of sts only dec 1 st at neck edge
of next 20 rows (24 sts).
Cont straight until Front matches Back, ending at
armhole edge.

MATERIALS

- 25 g **Pale rose lightweight DK**
- 25 g **Rose madder lightweight DK**
- 50 g **Milkshake fine cotton chenille**
- 50 g **Cornflower fine cotton chenille**
- 25 g **Magenta lightweight DK**
- 50 g **Crocus fine cotton chenille**
- 50 g **Plum fine cotton chenille**
- 2 x 25 g **Smoke lightweight DK**
- 9 x 50 g **Charcoal DDK**
- 1 pair 3¼-mm (US 3, UK 10) **needles**
- 1 pair 4-mm (US 6, UK 8) **needles**
- 1 set of four 3¼-mm (US 3, UK 10) **double-pointed needles**
- 3 stitch holders

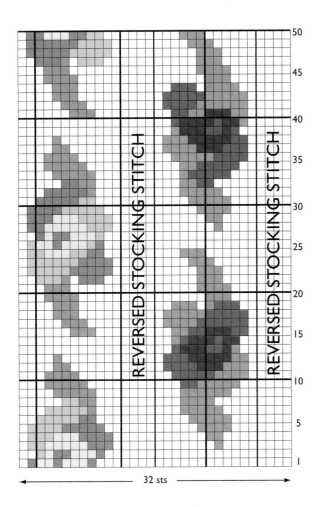

REVERSED STOCKING STITCH

REVERSED STOCKING STITCH

50

45

40

35

30

25

20

15

10

5

1

← 32 sts →

Rose Rib Turtleneck Sweater

Color Key

☐ Pale rose

▨ Rose madder

▨ Milkshake

▨ Cornflower

▨ Magenta

▨ Crocus

▨ Plum

▨ Smoke

☐ Charcoal

Shoulder shaping: keeping continuity of patt bind off/cast off 8 sts at beg of foll 3 alt rows.

Return to sts on holder for second side and sl center 16 sts onto another holder. Rejoin yarn to rem sts with RS facing and patt to end. Work as for left side, reversing all shapings.

SLEEVES

With 3¼-mm needles and Charcoal cast on 50 sts.
Work 2½'' K2 P2 rib, inc 1 st at both ends of last row.
Change to 4-mm needles and foll chart from bottom to top, and **at the same time,** inc 1 st at both ends of next and every foll 3rd row until there are 108 sts, taking extra sts into patt as they occur.
Cont straight until Sleeve measures 18'' from cast-on edge.
Shape top: keeping continuity of patt bind off/cast off 6 sts at beg of next 2 rows.
Dec 1 st at both ends of next 6 rows.
Patt 2 rows.

Bind off/cast off 19 sts at beg of next 2 rows.
Patt 2 rows.
Bind off/cast off 14 sts at beg of next 2 rows and rem 18 sts at beg of foll row.

COLLAR

Join shoulder seams.
With a set of four 3¼-mm double-pointed needles and Charcoal and RS facing, pick up and K 1 st for each row along Left Front neck, K across 16 sts at Front neck, K 1 st for each row up Right Front neck, then K across 56 sts across Back neck.
Work 8'' in K2 P2 rib.
Bind off/cast off in rib.

MAKING UP

Tidy loose ends back into their own colors. Join Sleeve and side seams. Sew Sleeve into armhole. Press lightly with a warm iron over a damp cloth, omitting ribbings.

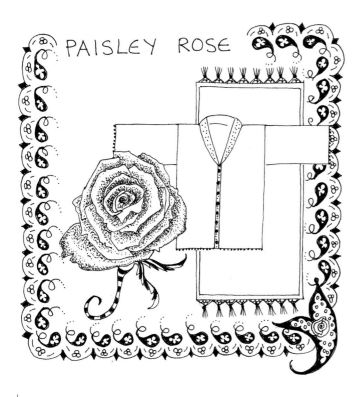

PAISLEY ROSE

Paisley Rose Jacket

Actual measurements:
bust 51", center back neck to welt 29",
sleeve seam 16"

Gauge/tension:
24 sts and 32 rows to 4" on
3¾-mm needles over patt

INSTRUCTIONS

BACK

With 2¾-mm needles and Black cast on 153 sts.
Work 4 rows st st.
Next row: work a picot edge: K1 (yfwd K2 tog) to end.
Next row: P.
Change to 3¾-mm needles and foll chart from bottom to top once and then rep Row 60 to Row 100 until work measures 28" from picot edge line.
Shoulder shaping: bind off/cast off 19 sts at beg of next 2 rows and 20 sts at beg of foll 4 rows.
Bind off/cast off rem 35 sts.

LEFT FRONT

With 2¾-mm needles and Black cast on 75 sts.
Work 4 rows st st.
Work picot edge as for Back.
Change to 3¾-mm needles and foll chart from bottom to top once and then rep Row 60 to Row 100 until 128 rows have been worked in all.
Shape front slope: dec 1 st at neck edge of next row and at same edge on every foll 4th row until there are 59 sts.
Cont without further shaping until Front measures same as Back to shoulder shaping, ending at shoulder edge.
Shoulder shaping: bind off/cast off 19 sts at beg of next row and 20 sts at beg of foll 2 alt rows.

MATERIALS

- **25 g Rose madder lightweight DK**
- **50 g Ruby fine cotton chenille**
- **2 x 25 g Rose lightweight DK**
- **2 x 25 g Vermilion lightweight DK**
- **2 x 25 g Pale rose lightweight DK**
- **25 g Oriental blue lightweight DK**
- **50 g Privet fine cotton chenille**
- **3 x 25 g Violet carmine lightweight DK**
- **2 x 25g Teal green lightweight DK**
- **2 x 25 g Rust lightweight DK**
- **10 x 50 g Black DDK**
- **1 pair 2¾-mm (US 2, UK 12) needles**
- **1 pair 3¾-mm (US 5, UK 9) needles**
- **8 buttons**

RIGHT FRONT

Work as for Left Front, reversing all shapings and starting at st 24 of chart.

SLEEVES

With 2¾-mm needles and Black cast on 102 sts.

Work 4 rows st st.

Work picot edge as for Back.

Change to 3¾-mm needles and foll chart from bottom to top once and then rep Row 60 to Row 100 until Sleeve measures 16" from picot edge line.

Bind off/cast off.

LEFT FRONT BAND

Join shoulder seams.

With 2¾-mm needles and Black cast on 8 sts.

Work in seed st/moss st until Left Front Band is long enough when stretched a little to fit from picot edge line up to beg of front neck shaping, ending at inner front edge.

Shape collar: cont in seed st/moss st, inc 1 st at end of next row and every foll alt row until there are 26 sts.

Mark corresponding position of length of band on Right Front with a colored thread.

Work straight until collar fits to mark, ending at inner neck edge.

Cont in seed st/moss st, dec 1 st at end of next row and every foll alt row until 8 sts rem.

Place 8 button markers on Left Front Band, the first at 1 cm up from picot edge line and the last at beg of neck shaping; space rem buttons evenly between.

RIGHT FRONT BAND

Cont in seed st/moss st as set, and **at the same time,** make buttonholes to correspond with button markers on Left Front Band as foll:

Row 1: seed st/moss 3, bind off/cast off 2, seed st/moss to end.

Row 2: seed st/moss to end, casting on 2 sts in place of the bound-off/cast-off sts in previous row.

Cont in this way until Right Front Band matches Left Front Band to picot edge line.

Bind off/cast off in seed st/moss st.

MAKING UP

Tidy loose ends back into their own colors. Position top of Sleeve so that center is at shoulder seam and sew in place. Join Sleeve and side seams. Attach Front Band and Collar. Fold back facings at picot edges on welt and Sleeves, and hem into place. Sew on buttons to match buttonholes. Press lightly with a warm iron over a damp cloth.

Paisley Rose Jacket and Throw

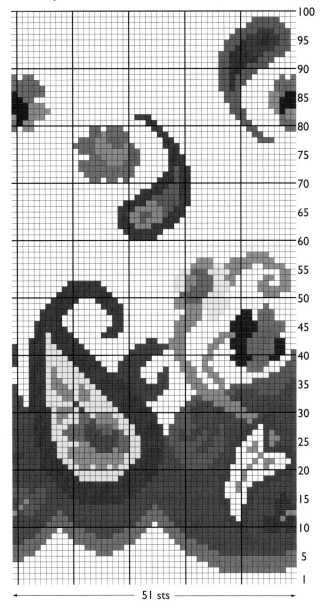

51 sts

Color Key

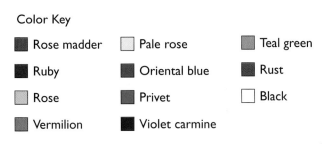

- Rose madder
- Ruby
- Rose
- Vermilion
- Pale rose
- Oriental blue
- Privet
- Violet carmine
- Teal green
- Rust
- Black

Paisley Rose Throw

Actual measurements:
36" × 56"

Gauge/tension:
24 sts and 28 rows to 4" on
4-mm needles over intarsia

INSTRUCTIONS

With 3¼-mm needles and Black cast on 204 sts.
Work 1" seed st/moss st.
Change to 4¼-mm needles and foll chart from bottom
to top once (100 rows), then again from Row 61 to
Row 100 four more times.

Now work from Row 59 to Row 83, leaving out the
beg of Green swirl and its rose (231 rows of chart
altogether).
Turn chart upside down and foll chart from Row 58
down to Row 1 (289 rows altogether).
Change to 3¼-mm needles and then work 1" seed
st/moss st.
Bind off/cast off.

SIDE NEATENINGS

With 3¼-mm needles and Black pick up and K 1 st
for each row along side edge of throw.
Work 1" seed st/moss st.
Bind off/cast off.
Work other side to match.

CROCHET BORDER

Row 1: with 1.50-mm crochet hook and Black work
sc/dc along bottom edge of throw.
Row 2: work 1 row hdc/htr with Violet carmine.

MATERIALS

- 2 x 25 g Rose madder lightweight DK
- 50 g Ruby fine cotton chenille
- 25 g Rose lightweight DK
- 2 x 25 g Vermilion lightweight
  DK
- 25 g Pale rose lightweight DK
- 2 x 25 g Oriental blue lightweight DK
- 50 g Privet fine cotton
  chenille
- 4 x 25 g Violet carmine lightweight DK
- 3 x 25 g Teal green lightweight
  DK
- 2 x 25 g Rust lightweight DK
- 12 x 50 g Black DDK
- 1 pair 3¼-mm (US 3, UK 10)
  needles
- 1 pair 4-mm (US 6, UK 8)
  needles
- 1.50-mm (US 6 steel, UK 12)
  crochet hook

Row 3: work 1 row hdc/htr with Rose madder.
Row 4: work 1 row hdc/htr with Oriental blue.
Row 5: work 1 row sc/dc with Violet carmine.
Row 6: work 1 row sc/dc with Rose madder.
Row 7: work 1 row sc/dc with Oriental blue.
Row 8: work 1 row sc/dc with Black.
Divide base of throw into 8 even sections and place a marker at beg of each section.

Section 1: with RS facing join in Black to right corner of throw. 3 ch (counts as 1 hdc/htr) *5 ch, 1 hdc/htr (into 3rd st along)*. Rep from * to * 5 more times (6 ch loops altogether) turn.
Sl st 2 sts up side of end ch loop, 5 ch, 1 hdc/htr into center of 2nd loop *5 ch, 1 hdc/htr into center of next ch loop along*. Rep from * to * 3 more times, turn.

Cont in this patt until 1 loop rem. Fasten off.

Rep Section 1 seven more times, making 8 crochet triangles.

Make 4 Violet carmine large tassels with Ruby heads and 4 Teal green large tassels with Privet heads. (See "Techniques," p. 168.)

Attach tassels to points of triangles, placing Violet and Teal tassels alternately.

Rep crochet border instructions for top edge of throw. Tidy up loose ends back into their own color. Press lightly with a warm iron over a damp cloth.

Rosebud Cropped Top

Actual measurements:
bust 39", center back neck to
welt 18", sleeve seam 15½"

Gauge/tension:
27 sts and 32 rows to 4" on
3¾-mm needles over patt

INSTRUCTIONS

BACK

With 2¾-mm needles and Mint cast on 396 sts.
Work frill as foll:
Row 1: (K7 P2) 44 times.
Row 2: (K2 P7) 44 times.
Row 3: (sl 1 K1 psso K3 K2 tog P2) 44 times
(308 sts).
Row 4: (K2 P5) 44 times.
Row 5: (sl 1 K1 psso K1 K2 tog P2) 44 times
(220 sts).
Row 6: (K2 P3) 44 times.
Row 7: (sl 1 K2 tog psso P2) 44 times (132 sts).
Row 8: (K2 P1) 44 times.
Change to 3¾-mm needles and foll chart from bottom
to top until work measures 9" from cast-on edge.
Armhole shaping: keeping continuity of patt bind
off/cast off 8 sts at beg of next 2 rows (116 sts).
Cont straight until armhole measures 8½" ending with
a P row.
Shoulder shaping: keeping continuity of patt bind
off/cast off 9 sts at beg of next 6 rows.
Place rem 62 sts onto a stitch holder.

MATERIALS

- **50 g Ecru cotton glacé**
- **50 g Privet fine cotton chenille**
- **50 g Robin fine cotton chenille**
- **25 g Peach lightweight DK**
- **50 g Crushed rose cotton glacé**
- **25 g Pale rose lightweight DK**
- **10 x 50 g Mint cotton glacé**
- **I pair 2¾-mm (US 2, UK 12) needles**
- **I pair 3¾-mm (US 5, UK 9) needles**
- **I set of four 3¼-mm (US 3, UK 10) double-pointed needles**
- **2 stitch holders**

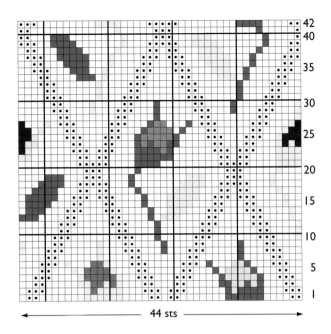

44 sts

Rosebud Cropped Top

Color Key

☐ Ecru

■ Privet

■ Robin

■ Peach

■ Crushed rose

☐ Pale rose

⊡ Mint (reversed st st)

☐ Mint

FRONT

Work as for Back until work measures 11½" from cast-on edge ending with a P row.

Neck shaping: patt 52 sts, turn, and place rem sts on a stitch holder.

Work each side of neck separately.

Working on rem sts only dec 1 st at neck edge on foll 15 rows.

Then dec 1 st at neck edge on foll 10 alt rows (27 sts).

Cont straight until Front matches Back to shoulder.

Shoulder shaping: keeping continuity of patt bind off/cast off 9 sts at beg of foll 3 alt rows.

Rejoin yarn to sts on stitch holder with RS facing, place next 12 sts onto a stitch holder and patt to end. Then work right side to match left side, reversing shapings.

SLEEVES

With 2¾-mm needles and Mint cast on 180 sts and work frill as foll:

Row 1: (K7 P2) 20 times.

Row 2: (K2 P7) 20 times.

Row 3: (sl 1 K1 psso K3 K2 tog P2) 20 times (140 sts).

Row 4: (K2 P5) 20 times.

Row 5: (sl 1 K1 psso K1 K2 tog P2) 20 times (100 sts).

Row 6: (K2 P3) 20 times.

Row 7: (sl 1 K2tog psso P2) 20 times (60 sts).

Row 8: (K2 P1) 20 times.

Change to 3¾-mm needles and foll chart twice, and **at the same time,** inc 1 st at both ends of next and every foll 4th row until there are 114 sts.

Change to Mint and P 1 row.

Then work 1" K1 P1 twisted rib.

Bind off/cast off in rib.

NECKBAND

Join shoulder seams.

With 1 set of four 3¾-mm double-pointed needles and Mint and RS facing, pick up and K 1 st for each row down left side of neck, across 12 sts on stitch holder, up right side of neck, and across 62 sts of back neck.

Work 3 rounds in st st.

Next round: work a picot edge: (yfwd K2 tog) to end of round.

Work 4 more rounds st st.

Bind off/cast off loosely.

MAKING UP

Tidy loose ends back into their own colors. Sew bound-off/cast-off edge of Sleeve top into armhole, the straight sides at top of Sleeve to form a neat right angle at bound-off/cast-off sts of armhole at Back and Front. Join rest of Sleeve and side seams. Fold Neckband facing to inside at picot edge and hem down. Press lightly with a warm iron over a damp cloth, omitting frill.

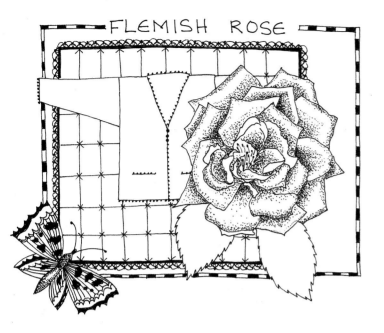

Flemish Rose Bedcover

Actual measurements:
58" × 74"

Gauge/tension:
26 sts and 32 rows to 4" on
3¾-mm needles over patt

INSTRUCTIONS

BASIC PATCH
With 3¾-mm needles and Oyster cast on 54 sts.
Foll chart from bottom to top once.
Bind off/cast off.

CROCHET BORDER
Round 1: starting at top right corner of patch with
1.50-mm crochet hook and Oyster work 52 sc/dc
(1 for each st) across top of patch, make 3 sc/dc into
corner st. Work in sc/dc along left side of patch as
foll: *2 sc/dc (1 for each st) skip/miss 1 st*. Rep from
* to * to bottom left corner (33 sts). Make 3 sc/dc into corner st. Work along bottom of patch, making 52
sc/dc (as for top). Make 3 sc/dc into corner st. Work
up right side of patch, making 33 sts as for left side.
Make 3 sc/dc into corner st. Join to 1st st.
Fasten off.
Round 2: attach Butter to right corner, make 3 ch
(count as 1 hdc/htr and 1 ch) *1 hdc/htr into 2nd st
along, 1 ch*. Rep from * to * to left corner. 1 hdc/htr
into center st of previous row's sc/dc, 3 ch, work next
hdc/htr into the same corner st (work forms a right
angle). Work left side, base, and right side as for top.
Join to beg of row.
Fasten off.

Round 3: attach Kiwi into ch st (between 2 hdc/htr) at right corner. Make 3 ch (count as 1 hdc/htr and 1 ch) *1 hdc/htr into 2nd ch along (insert hook into middle of ch), 1 ch*. Rep from * to * to left corner. 1 hdc/htr into center of previous row's 3 ch, 3 ch, work next hdc/htr into the same st (work forms a right angle). Work left side, base, and right side as for top. Join to beg of row.
Fasten off.
Round 4: work as for Round 3 using Pear.
Make 40 patches.

CONSTRUCTION

With a 1.50-mm crochet hook and Pear join patches tog with sc/dc, placing patches alternately right way up and upside down, as shown at right.

BORDER

Round 1: with 1.50-mm crochet hook and Pear work in sc/dc around 4 sides of bedcover, making 3 sc/dc into each corner.
Join to beg of row.
Fasten off.
Round 2, Shell Edging: with Butter 1 sl st *skip/miss 2 sts, 5 dc/tr into next st, skip/miss 2 sts, 1 sl st into next st. Rep from * around 4 sides of bedcover, making 8 dc/tr into corner sts.
Round 3, Picot Trim: with Butter join yarn into top of a shell *3 ch, sl st into same st, 5 ch, sl st into top of next shell*. Rep from * to * around 4 sides of bedcover.
Tidy loose ends back into their own colors. Press lightly on WS with a warm iron over a damp cloth.

Construction Diagram

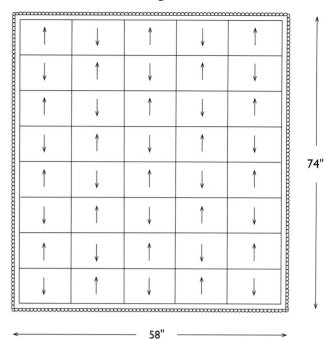

74"

58"

Arrows indicate direction of knitted patch.

Color Key

■	Petunia	■	Pear
■	Racy (use double)	■	Kiwi
■	Dusk	⊡	White
■	Hyacinth	☐	Butter
■	Lilac/Wine	☐	Oyster
■	Vine (use double)		

Flemish Rose Bedcover

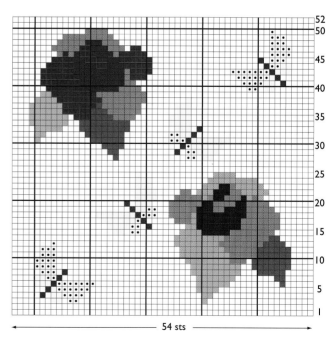

54 sts

Flemish Rose V-Neck Jacket

Actual measurements:
bust 46", center back neck to welt 32",
sleeve seam 14½"

Gauge/tension:
28 sts and 32 rows to 4" on
3¼-mm needles over patt

MATERIALS

- 2 x 25 g Pale yellow light-weight DK
- 25 g Mustard wool/silk
- 25 g Mole fine cotton chenille
- 25 g Bottle green wool/silk
- 25 g Willow fine cotton chenille
- 25 g Olive green wool/silk
- 50 g Catkin fine cotton chenille
- 25 g Plum fine cotton chenille
- 50 g Garnet wool/silk
- 50 g Pink fine cotton chenille
- 50 g Robin fine cotton chenille
- 50 g Oak fine cotton chenille
- 50 g Apricot wool/silk
- 9 x 50 g Ecru wool/silk
- 1 pair 3¼-mm (US 3, UK 10) needles
- 3.00-mm (US D/3, UK 9) crochet hook
- 2 stitch holders
- 3 buttons

INSTRUCTIONS

BACK

With 3¼-mm needles and Ecru cast on 162 sts.
Foll chart from bottom to top twice and again from
Row 1 to Row 50 (250 rows).
Shape shoulders: with Ecru only, bind off/cast off
18 sts at beg of next 6 rows.
Bind off/cast off rem 54 sts.

FRONTS

Beg by making 2 pocket linings. With 3¼-mm needles
and Ecru cast on 36 sts.
Work 6" st st. Place sts onto a stitch holder.

LEFT FRONT

With 3¼-mm needles and Ecru, cast on 81 sts.
Foll chart from bottom up to end of Row 51.
Row 52, place pocket: patt 22 sts, bind off/cast off
36 sts, patt 23 sts.
Row 53: patt 23 sts, work across 36 sts of pocket lin-
ing, patt 22 sts.
Cont until Front measures 18½" from cast-on edge,
ending with a RS row.

Flemish Rose V-Neck Jacket

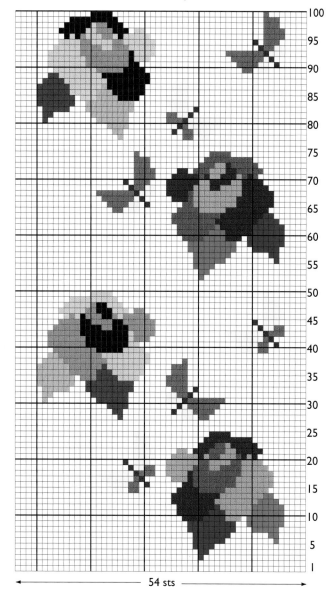

54 sts

Color Key

☐	Pale yellow	◼	Plum
◼	Mustard	◼	Garnet
◼	Mole	☐	Pink
◼	Bottle green	◼	Robin
◼	Willow	◼	Oak
◼	Olive green	◼	Apricot
◼	Catkin	☐	Ecru

Dec 1 st at neck edge on 3rd row and every foll 4th row until 54 sts rem.

Cont without further shaping until Front matches Back to shoulder.

Shape shoulder: with Ecru only bind off/cast off 18 sts at beg of next 3 alt rows.

RIGHT FRONT

Work as for Left Front, reversing all shapings and starting Row 1 of chart with a P row to give a mirror image.

SLEEVES

With 3¼-mm needles and Ecru cast on 62 sts. Beg patt at st 51 and foll chart, increasing 1 st at both ends of 3rd row and every foll 4th row until there are 138 sts, taking extra sts into patt as they occur.

Bind off/cast off.

MAKING UP

Tidy loose ends back into their own colors. Join shoulder seams. Position top of Sleeve so that center is at shoulder seam and sew in place. Join side and Sleeve seams. Sew down pocket linings. Press lightly with a warm iron over a damp cloth.

PICOT EDGING

With 3.00-mm crochet hook and Ecru and RS facing, work 1 row sc/dc starting at center back neck, down Left Front, around base, and up Right Front to center back neck.

Next row: work 1 ch *work 1 sc/dc into next st, 3 ch, 1 sc/dc into same place, work 3 sc/dc into next 3 sts*. Rep from * to * to end.

Work picot edging around cuffs and across pocket tops.

Attach 3 buttons opposite the first 3 picot loops at V point of neck.

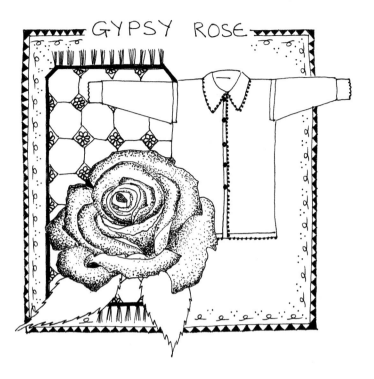

Gypsy Rose Coat

Actual measurements:
bust 48", center back neck to welt 32",
sleeve seam 15"

Gauge/tension:
19 sts and 24 rows to 4" on
4½-mm needles over patt

INSTRUCTIONS

SPECIAL INSTRUCTIONS:
INDIVIDUAL MOTIFS

Worked as intarsia method, except background yarn is not carried across back of motif. For this patt, rose should be worked as an individual motif.

BACK

With 3¼-mm needles and Dark blue skye cast on 114 sts.
Work 6 rows st st.
Change to Dark blue chenille and, with RS facing, work a picot edge: K1 (yfwd K2 tog) to last st, K1.
Work 5 rows st st, starting with a P row.
Change to 4½-mm needles and Dark blue skye and foll chart from bottom to top for 116 rows.
Row 117, armhole shaping: keeping continuity of patt bind off/cast off 6 sts at beg of next 2 rows.
Cont straight to and including Row 64 of second working of chart.
Shape shoulders: using Dark blue skye only bind off/cast off 12 sts at beg of next 6 rows.
Bind off/cast off rem 30 sts.

MATERIALS

All yarns by Collinette

- 7 x 100 g Dark blue skye
- 100 g Pale olive chenille
- 100 g Dark purple chenille
- 100 g Pale blue chenille
- 2 x 100 g Dark blue chenille
- 2 x 100 g Lapis lazuli salsa
- 1 pair 3¼-mm (US 3, UK 10) needles
- 1 pair 3¾-mm (US 5, UK 9) needles
- 1 pair 4½-mm (US 7, UK 7) needles
- 5 buttons

LEFT FRONT

With 3¼-mm needles and Dark blue skye cast on 56 sts.

Work 6 rows st st.

Change to Dark blue chenille and, with RS facing, work a picot edge: K1 (yfwd K2 tog) to last st, K1.

Work 5 rows st st, starting with a P row; inc 1 st at center of last row (57 sts).

Change to 4½-mm needles and Dark blue skye and foll chart from bottom to top for 116 rows.

Row 117, armhole shaping: keeping continuity of patt bind off/cast off 6 sts at beg of row.

Cont straight to Row 45 of second working of chart.

Row 46, neck shaping: bind off/cast off 5 sts at beg of row.

Keeping continuity of patt, dec 1 st at neck edge on next and every foll row until 36 sts rem.

Cont straight to match Back, ending with a P row.

Shoulder shaping: using Dark blue skye only bind off/cast off 12 sts at beg of next 3 alt rows.

RIGHT FRONT

Work as for Left Front, reversing all shapings.

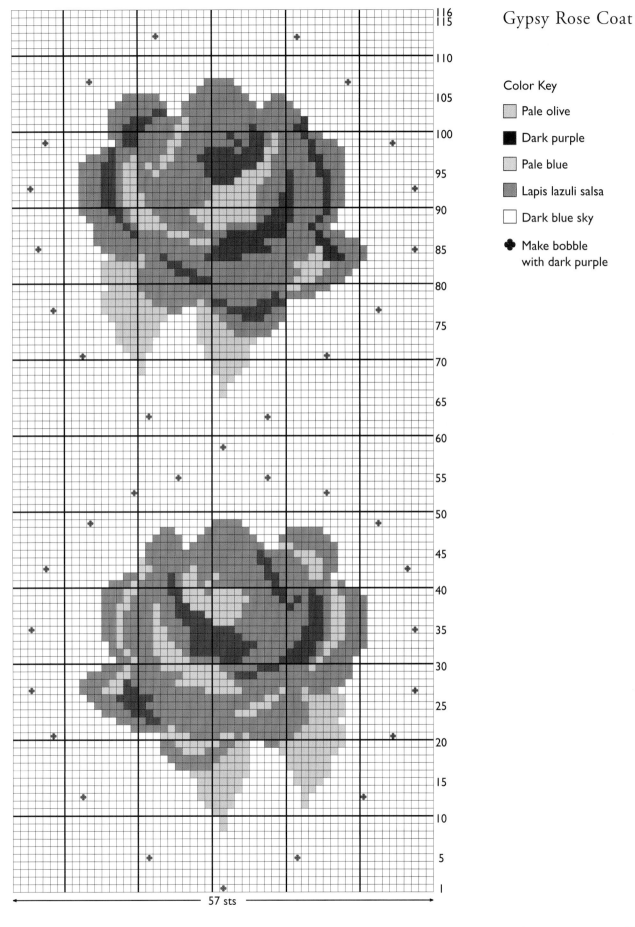

Gypsy Rose Coat

Color Key

Pale olive

Dark purple

Pale blue

Lapis lazuli salsa

Dark blue sky

♣ Make bobble
with dark purple

57 sts

SLEEVES

With 3¼-mm needles and Dark blue chenille, cast on 56 sts.

Work 3½" st st, ending with a P row.

Next row: work a picot edge as for Back, then work 3½" st st, starting and ending with a P row; inc 1 st at center of last row (57 sts).

Change to 4½-mm needles and Dark blue skye and foll chart from bottom to top up to and including Row 64, and **at the same time,** inc 1 st at both ends of next and every foll 4th row (89 sts).

Change to 3¼-mm needles and Dark blue chenille and work 12 rows st st.

Change to 4½-mm needles and Dark blue skye, K 1 row, then bind off/cast off loosely.

LEFT FRONT BAND

With 3¾-mm needles and Dark blue skye and RS facing, pick up and K 1 st for each row along Left Front from neck to picot fold line.

Work 5 rows K1 P1 twisted rib.

Change to 3¼-mm needles and Dark blue chenille, work 2 rows st st.

Work a picot edge as for Back.

P 1 row.

Bind off/cast off.

RIGHT FRONT BAND

Work as for Left Front Band but on Row 4 work 5 evenly spaced buttonholes, the first hole 9" from welt and the last hole 3 sts from neck, binding off/casting off 3 sts for each hole and casting on 3 sts over the bound-off/cast-off sts on next row.

COLLAR

Join shoulder seams.

With 3¼-mm needles and Dark blue chenille and RS facing, pick up and K 88 sts round neck starting halfway across Right Front Band and ending halfway across Left Front Band.

Work 2 rows st st starting with a K row.

Next row (inc row): K2, yfwd, K to last 2 sts, yfwd, K2.

Cont in st st working the inc row on every 4th row until 8 increases have been made (105 sts).

Then work 2 inc rows on next 2 alt K rows (108 sts).

P 1 row.

Next row: work a picot edge as for Back.

P 1 row.

Next row (dec row): K2, yfwd, (sl 1 K1 psso) twice, K to last 6 sts (K2 tog) twice, yfwd, K2.

Cont in st st working the dec row on next 2 alt rows and then on every 4th row until there are 88 sts.

P 1 row.

Bind off/cast off loosely knitwise.

MAKING UP

Tidy loose ends back into their own colors. Fold collar at picot edge with RS tog, oversew side edges, turn inside out and hem to neck. Fold picot edge of Front Bands to WS and hem down, making sure you avoid covering buttonholes on Right Front Band. Sew bound-off/cast-off edge of Sleeve top into armhole, the straight sides at top of Sleeve to form a neat right angle at bound-off/cast-off sts of armhole at Front and Back. Join rest of Sleeve and side seams. Fold welts at picot edge to WS and hem down. Fold cuff at picot edge to WS and hem down. Sew on buttons to match buttonholes. Press lightly with a warm iron over a damp cloth.

Gypsy Rose Throw

Actual measurements:
34" × 50"

Gauge/tension:
28 sts and 24 rows to 1" on
3¾-mm needles over patt

MATERIALS

- **25 g Cobalt green lightweight DK**
- **2 x 25 g Mistletoe green lightweight DK**
- **50 g Ruby fine cotton chenille**
- **50 g Plum fine cotton chenille**
- **25 g Geranium lightweight DK**
- **8 x 25 g Mist Donegal lambswool tweed**
- **25 g Pale olive green lightweight DK**
- **25 g Violet lightweight DK**
- **25 g Light purple lightweight DK**
- **10 x 25 g Bluebell lightweight DK**
- **7 x 50 g Black DDK**
- **1 pair 3¾-mm (US 5, UK 9) needles**
- **1.50-mm (US 6 steel, UK 12) crochet hook**

INSTRUCTIONS

OCTAGON

With 3¾-mm needles and main color cast on 24 sts. Inc 1 st at beg and end of every row until 48 sts, and **at the same time,** foll rose design as on chart, being careful not to let background yarn pull as it is woven in behind motif.

Row 47: dec 1 st at both ends of every row until 24 sts rem.

Bind off/cast off.

Make 12 octagons from chart A and 12 octagons from chart B.

OCTAGON CROCHET BORDERS
MIST OCTAGONS

Row 1: with 1.50-mm crochet hook and Mist work in sc/dc around 8 sides of octagon, making 3 sts in each corner.

Row 2: with Mistletoe green work in sc/dc around octagon, making 3 sts in center st of each corner. When working this and foll rows of sc/dc, put hook into back 2 loops of st to form a ridge of color at the front.

Row 3: with Black work 1 row sc/dc as for Row 2.

BLACK OCTAGONS

Work as for Mist Octagons in foll colors:

Row 1: Black.

Row 2: Bluebell.

Row 3: Black.

IRISH CROCHET ROSES

With 1.5-mm crochet hook and Bluebell make 7 ch, sl st into 1st ch to form a ring.

Round 1: 1 ch, work 16 sc/dc into ring, sl st into 1st sc/dc.

Round 2: 1 ch, 1 sc/dc, into 1st sc/dc (5 ch, skip/miss 1 sc/dc, 1 sc/dc into next sc/dc) 7 times, 5 ch, sl st into 1st sc/dc.

Round 3: sl st, into 1st 5-ch arch, 1 ch, work

(1 sc/dc, 5 hdc/htr, 1 sc/dc) into each 5-ch arch to end, sl st into 1st sc/dc (8 petals).

Make 15 roses.

IRISH CROCHET HALF-ROSES

Row 1: with 1.50-mm crochet hook and Bluebell make 7 ch.

Row 2: make 5 dc/tr into 4th ch from beg, sl st into last ch (7 dc/tr) turn.

Row 3: 5 ch, sc/dc into 2nd st, *5 ch, sc/dc into 4th st*. Rep from * to * to end (4 loops), skip/miss 1st st each time before making sc/dc. Turn.

Row 4: 1 ch, work (1 sc/dc, 5 hdc/htr, 1 sc/dc) into each 5-ch arch to end (4 petals).

Make 16 half-roses.

CONSTRUCTION

With Bluebell join Black and Mist Octagons tog with sc/dc as shown at left.

Row 1: with 1.50-mm crochet hook and Bluebell sc/dc around center diamonds, dec 1 st at each corner.

Row 2: as Row 1.

Row 3: work as for Row 1, catching outside of rose petals with a sl st; attach 2 petals onto each side of diamond.

Join half-roses onto half-diamonds on outside of throw, as shown at left, dec 1 st at V point and outside edges.

Join Bluebell onto RS of half-diamond, sc/dc across ends of 3 rows; sc/dc, 3 ch, sc/dc across half-rose; 3 ch sc/dc across ends of 3 rows; sc/dc. Fasten off.

BORDER

Row 1: with 1.50-mm crochet hook and Black work sc/dc around 4 sides of throw.

Row 2: with Black work hdc/htr around 4 sides of throw.

Work 3 rows hdc/htr at top and bottom of throw. Make sixty-six 4" small tassels (see "Techniques," p. 168) in Black and attach 33 to top of throw and 33 to bottom of throw.

Tidy loose ends back into their own colors. Press lightly with a warm iron over a damp cloth.

Construction Diagram

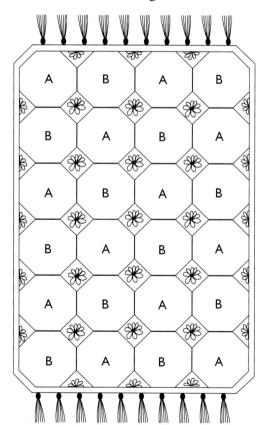

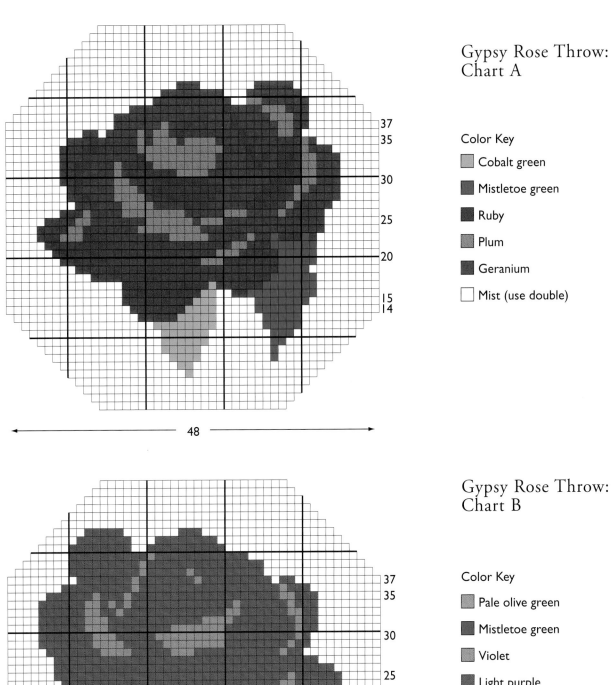

Gypsy Rose Throw: Chart A

37
35

30

25

20

15
14

Color Key

Cobalt green

Mistletoe green

Ruby

Plum

Geranium

Mist (use double)

← 48 →

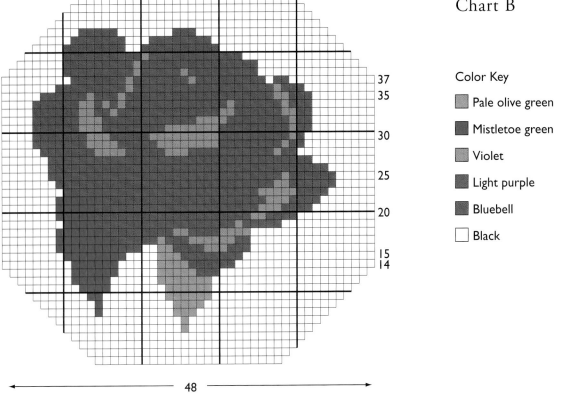

Gypsy Rose Throw: Chart B

37
35

30

25

20

15
14

Color Key

Pale olive green

Mistletoe green

Violet

Light purple

Bluebell

Black

← 48 →

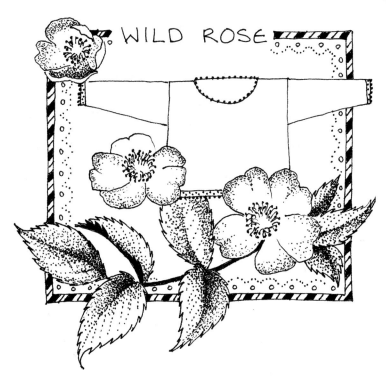

Wild Rose Top

Actual measurements:
bust 40", center back neck to welt 21",
sleeve seam 19½"

Gauge/tension:
27 sts and 32 rows to 4" on
3¼-mm needles over patt

MATERIALS

- 25 g Tarragon Donegal lambs-wool tweed
- 50 g Garnet wool/silk
- 25 g Rose lightweight DK
- 50 g Milkshake fine cotton chenille
- 2 x 25 g Dark peach lightweight DK
- 25 g Rust lightweight DK
- 50 g Robin fine cotton chenille
- 5 x 50 g Ecru wool/silk
- 50 g Catkin fine cotton chenille
- 25 g Leaf Donegal lambswool tweed
- 25 g Pale yellow lightweight DK
- I pair 2¾-mm (US 2, UK 12) needles
- I pair 3¼-mm (US 3, UK 10) needles
- I set of four 2¾-mm (US 2, UK 12) double-pointed needles
- 2.00-mm (US B/I, UK 10) crochet hook
- I stitch holder

INSTRUCTIONS

BACK

With 2¾-mm needles and Ecru cast on 148 sts.
Work 6 rows seed st/moss st.
Change to 3¼-mm needles and foll chart from bottom to top 2½ times (170 rows).
Shoulder shaping: using Ecru only bind off/cast off 41 sts at beg of next 2 rows.
Bind off/cast off rem 66 sts.

FRONT

Work as for Back until work measures 16½" from cast-on edge ending with a P row.
Neck shaping: patt 68 sts, turn and place rem sts onto a stitch holder.
Work each side of neck separately.
Bind off/cast off at beg of next row and foll alt rows:
5 sts once, 4 sts twice, 3 sts twice, 2 sts twice, and 1 st 4 times (41 sts).
Cont straight until Front matches Back to shoulder.
Bind off/cast off rem 41 sts.
With RS facing, rejoin yarn to sts on holder, bind off/cast off center 12 sts, patt to end.
Work 1 row then complete second side to match first side, reversing all shapings.

Wild Rose Top

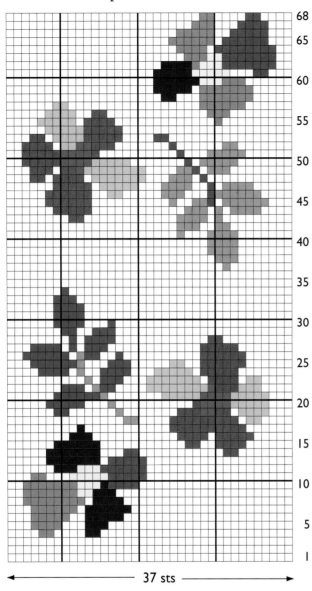

68
65
60
55
50
45
40
35
30
25
20
15
10
5
1

← 37 sts →

Color Key

Catkin

Leaf

Pale yellow

Tarragon

Garnet

Rose

Milkshake

Dark peach

Rust

Robin

Ecru

SLEEVES

With 2¾-mm needles and Ecru cast on 59 sts.

Work 6 rows seed st/moss st.

Change to 3¼-mm needles and foll chart from bottom to top twice, starting at st 11, and **at the same time,** shape sides by inc 1 st at both ends of next and every 5th row until there are 115 sts, taking extra sts into patt as they occur.

Work 4 rows st st in Ecru.

Bind off/cast off.

NECKBAND

Join shoulder seams.

With a set of four 2¾-mm double-pointed needles, RS facing and Ecru pick up and K an even number of sts from center back neck, down left side of neck, across Front, up right side of neck, to center back neck.

Work 4 rows seed st/moss st.

Bind off/cast off in seed st/moss st.

MAKING UP

Tidy loose ends back into their own colors. Position Sleeves with center top to shoulder seam and sew in place. Join side and Sleeve seams. Press lightly with a warm iron over a damp cloth.

CROCHET PICOT TRIM

Round 1: with 2.00-mm crochet hook and Ecru join yarn to center back neck. Work 1 row sc/dc around neck.

Round 2: picot edge: *sl st along 3 sc/dc of previous row, 3 ch, sl st into same st*. Rep from * to * around neck.

Work these 2 rounds around cuffs and welt.

Cable Rose Round-Neck Cardigan

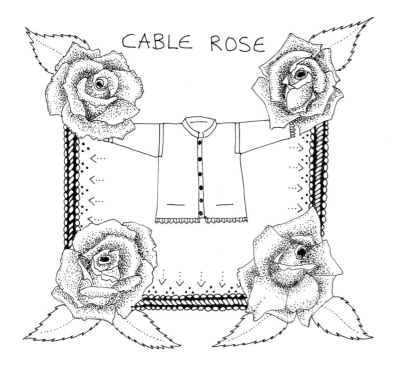

CABLE ROSE

Actual measurements:
bust 45", center back neck to welt 25",
sleeve seam 10"

Gauge/tension:
28 sts and 30 rows to 4" on
3¾-mm needles over patt

MATERIALS

- 50 g **Mint cotton glacé**
- 50 g **Provence cotton glacé**
- 50 g **Candy floss cotton glacé**
- 50 g **Magenta 4-ply cotton**
- 50 g **White cotton glacé**
- 50 g **Lilac/wine cotton glacé**
- 50 g **Fuchsia cotton glacé**
- 50 g **Crocus fine cotton chenille**
- 14 x 50 g **Oyster cotton glacé**
- 1 pair 3¼-mm **(US 3, UK 10) needles**
- 1 pair 3¾-mm **(US 5, UK 9) needles**
- cable needle
- 1 stitch holder
- 6 buttons

INSTRUCTIONS

BACK

With 3¼-mm needles and Oyster cast on 460 sts.
Work frill as foll:
Row 1: P1 (K7 P2) 51 times.
Row 2: (K2 P7) 51 times K1.
Row 3: P1 (sl 1 K1 psso, K3, K2 tog, P2) 51 times
(358 sts).
Row 4: (K2 P5) 51 times K1.
Row 5: P1 (sl 1 K1 psso, K1, K2 tog) 51 times
(256 sts).
Row 6: (K2 P3) 51 times K1.
Row 7: (sl 1 K2 tog psso, P2) 5 times (154 sts).
Row 8: (K2 P1) 51 times.
Change to 3¾-mm needles and foll chart from bottom
to top twice, up to and including Row 48 of second
working of chart.

Armhole shaping: keeping continuity of patt bind off/cast off 14 sts at beg of next 2 rows (126 sts). Cont straight until chart has been worked 3 times in all.
Change to Oyster and work 1" K1 P1 twisted rib.
Shoulder shaping: still in K1 P1 twisted rib bind off/cast off 14 sts at beg of next 6 rows.
Place rem 42 sts onto a stitch holder.

LEFT FRONT

With 3¾-mm needles and Oyster cast on 252 sts.
Work frill as foll:
Row 1: (K7 P2) 28 times.
Row 2: (K2 P7) 28 times.
Row 3: (sl 1 K1 psso, K3, K2 tog, P2) 28 times (196 sts).
Row 4: (K2 P5) 28 times.
Row 5: (sl 1 K1 psso, K1, K2 tog) 28 times (140 sts).
Row 6: (K2 P3) 28 times.
Row 7: (sl 1 K2 tog psso, P2) 28 times (84 sts).

Row 8: (K2 P1) 28 times.
Change to 3¾-mm needles and foll chart from bottom to top, starting at st 29 on Row 1, up to and including Row 26.
Row 27, introduce pocket: patt 28 then, working on next 28 sts only and with Oyster, work 7" in st st. Return to main work and complete Row 27.
Cont to Row 48 of second working of chart.
Row 49, armhole shaping: keeping continuity of patt bind off/cast off 14 sts at beg of row.
Cont straight to and including Row 35 of third working of chart.
Row 40, neck shaping: keeping continuity of patt bind off/cast off 8 sts at beg of row.
Then dec 1 st at neck edge on next 20 rows.
Change to Oyster and work 1" K1 P1 twisted rib.
Shoulder shaping: still in K1 P1 twisted rib bind off/cast off 14 sts at beg of next 3 alt rows.

RIGHT FRONT

Work as for Left Front, reversing all shapings, and starting chart at st 1 on Row 1.

SLEEVES

With 3¾-mm needles and Oyster cast on 234 sts.
Work frill as foll:
Row 1: (K7 P2) 26 times.
Row 2: (K2 P7) 26 times.
Row 3: (sl 1 K1 psso, K3, K2 tog, P2) 26 times (182 sts).
Row 4: (K2 P5) 26 times.
Row 5: (sl 1 K1 psso, K1, K2 tog) 26 times (130 sts).
Row 6: (K2 P3) 26 times.
Row 7: (sl 1 K2 tog psso, P2) 26 times (78 sts).
Row 8: (K2 P1) 26 times.
Change to 3¾-mm needles and foll chart 1¾ times (98 rows), and **at the same time,** inc 1 st at both ends of every foll 3rd row until there are 134 sts, taking extra stitches into patt as they occur.
Cont straight to and including Row 41 of second working of chart.
Bind off/cast off in patt.

LEFT FRONT BAND

With 3¾-mm needles and Oyster pick up and K 1 st for each row from neck to welt, not including frill.
Work 1" K1 P1 twisted rib.
Bind off/cast off in rib.

Cable Rose Round-Neck Cardigan

Color and Stitch Key

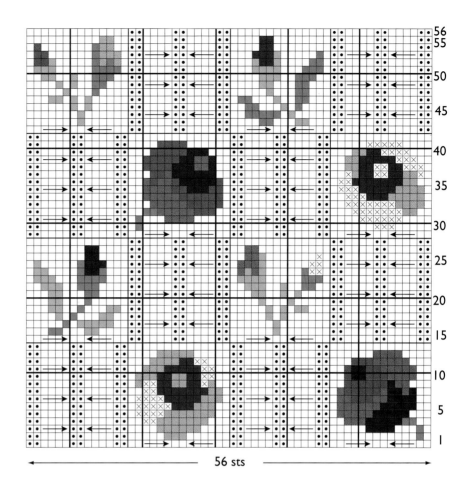

56 sts

	Mint
	Provence
	Candy floss
	Magenta (use double)
⊠	White
	Lilac/Wine
	Fuchsia
	Crocus
	Oyster
⊡	P in background color
◁———	Twist cable to left
———▷	Twist cable to right

RIGHT FRONT BAND

Work as for Left Front Band except work 6 button-holes evenly spaced along band on Row 3, binding off/casting off 3 sts for each hole and casting on 3 sts over the bound-off/cast-off sts on previous row. Complete as for Left Front Band.

NECKBAND

With 3¾-mm needles and Oyster and RS facing, pick up and K 1 st for each row or st from halfway across Right Front Band, up right neck, across 42 sts of back neck, down left neck, to halfway across Left Front Band.
Work 1" K1 P1 twisted rib.
Bind off/cast off in rib.

MAKING UP

Tidy loose ends back into their own colors. Sew bound-off/cast-off edge of sleeve top into armhole, the straight sides at top of Sleeve to form a neat right angle at bound-off/cast-off sts of armhole at Front and Back. Join rest of Sleeve and side seams. Join edges of pocket linings. Sew on buttons to match buttonholes. Press lightly with a warm iron over a damp cloth.

Autumn Leaves

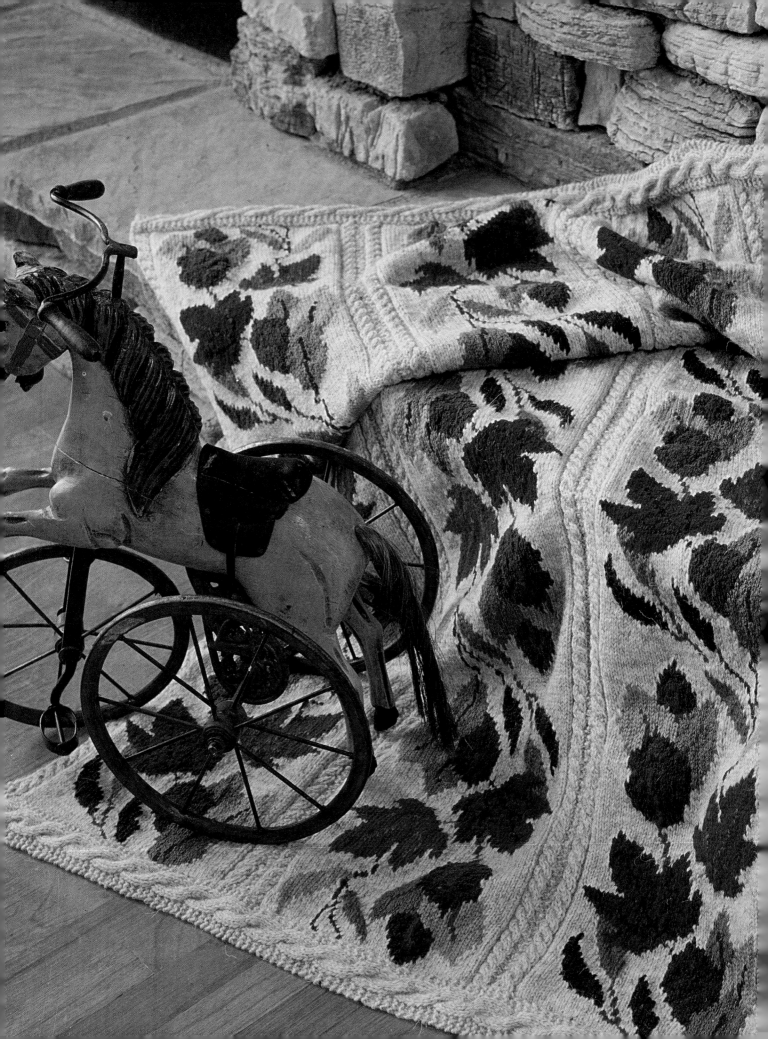

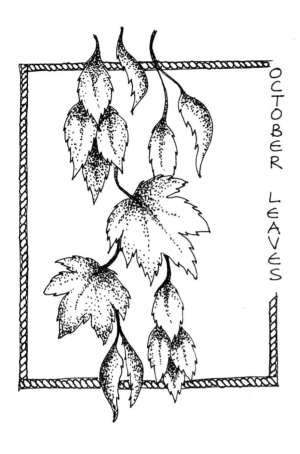

OCTOBER LEAVES

October Leaves Throw

Actual measurements:
69" × 48"

Gauge/tension:
20 sts and 24 rows to 4" on
4½-mm needles over patt

INSTRUCTIONS

Throw is made in four sections.

SECTION 1

With 4½-mm needles and Dapple cast on 66 sts.
Foll chart from bottom to top 4 times.
Bind off/cast off.
Make 3 more sections in the same manner.

CABLE BORDERS (MAKE TWO)

With 4½-mm needles and Dapple cast on 12 sts.
Work cable border as foll:
Rows 1, 3, and 5: K.
Rows 2, 4, and 6: K3 P6 K3.
Row 7: K3 C6 K3.
Rows 8 and 10: as Row 2.
Row 9: K.
Rep Row 1 to Row 10 until border measures 48".
Bind off/cast off.

MATERIALS

- 2 x 100 g Moss magpie Aran
- 100 g Fern chunky cotton chenille
- 100 g Laurel magpie Aran
- 2 x 50 g Marsh fine cotton chenille
- 2 x 100 g Chocolate chunky cotton chenille
- 100 g Maple chunky cotton chenille
- 2 x 100 g Lush chunky cotton chenille
- 12 x 100 g Dapple magpie Aran
- 1 pair 4½-mm (US 7, UK 7) needles
- cable needle

47

October Leaves Throw and Bolster

66 sts

Color Key

- Moss
- Fern
- Laurel
- Marsh (use double)
- Chocolate
- Maple
- Lush
- Dapple or Cloud (bolster background)
- P on K row, K on P row
- Twist cable to left
- Twist cable to right

CONSTRUCTION

Tidy loose ends back into their own colors. Sew
4 sections tog, alternating sections with design right
way up and upside down, as shown at right. Sew cable borders to top and bottom of throw.
Press lightly with a warm iron over a damp cloth.

Construction Diagram

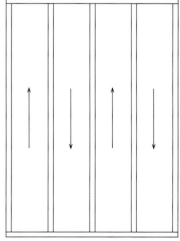

October Leaves Bolster

Actual measurements:
length 16", circumference 26½",
diameter 8½"

Gauge/tension:
20 sts and 24 rows to 4" on
4½-mm needles over patt

INSTRUCTIONS

BODY

With 4½-mm needles and Cloud cast on 132 sts.
Foll chart from bottom to top once weaving back-
ground yarn along behind each motif.
Bind off/cast off.

BOLSTER ENDS (MAKE TWO)

With a set of four 4½-mm double-pointed needles and
Cloud cast on 8 sts.
Round 1: (yo K1) to end of round.
Round 2: (yo K2 tog) to end of round.
Round 3: (yo K2) to end of round.
Round 4: (yo K1 K2 tog) to end of round.
Round 5: (yo K3) to end of round.
Round 6: (yo K2 K2 tog) to end of round.
Round 7: (yo K4) to end of round.
Round 8: (yo K3 K2 tog) to end of round.
Round 9: (yo K5) to end of round.
Round 10: (yo K4 K2 tog) to end of round.
Round 11: (yo K6) to end of round.

MATERIALS

- **100 g Moss magpie Aran**
- **100 g Fern chunky cotton chenille**
- **100 g Laurel magpie Aran**
- **50 g Marsh fine cotton chenille**
- **100 g Chocolate chunky cotton chenille**
- **100 g Maple chunky cotton chenille**
- **100 g Lush chunky cotton chenille**
- **2 x 100 g Cloud magpie Aran**
- **1 pair 4½-mm (US 7, UK 7) needles**
- **1 set of four 4½-mm (US 7, UK 7) double-pointed needles**
- **1 cylindrical cushion pad**

Round 12: (yo K5 K2 tog) to end of round.
Round 13: (yo K7) to end of round.
Round 14: (yo K6 K2 tog) to end of round.
Round 15: (yo K8) to end of round.
Round 16: (yo K7 K2 tog) to end of round.
Round 17: (yo K9) to end of round.
Round 18: (yo K8 K2 tog) to end of round.
Round 19: (yo K10) to end of round.
Round 20: (yo K9 K2 tog) to end of round.
Round 21: (yo K11) to end of round.
Round 22: (yo K10 K2 tog) to end of round.
Round 23: (yo K12) to end of round.
Round 24: (yo K11 K2 tog) to end of round.
Round 25: (yo K13) to end of round.
Round 26: (yo K12 K2 tog) to end of round.
Round 27: (yo K14) to end of round.
Round 28: (yo K13 K2 tog) to end of round.
Round 29: (yo K15) to end of round.

Round 30: (yo K14 K2 tog) to end of round.
Round 31: (yo K16) to end of round.
Round 32: (yo K15 K2 tog) to end of round.
Round 33: (yo K17) to end of round.
Round 34: (yo K16 K2 tog) to end of round
(144 sts).
Bind off/cast off.
Large tassel: make two 6" long large tassels using all
the chenille colors. (See "Techniques," p. 168.)

MAKING UP

Tidy loose ends back into their own colors. Press
pieces lightly with a warm iron over a damp cloth.
Attach tassels to center of bolster ends. Join cast-on
and bound-off/cast-off edges of body to form a cylin-
der. Place around cushion pad and sew bolster ends in
position.

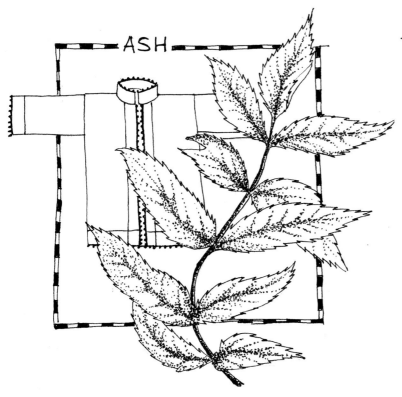

ASH

Ash Kimono

Actual measurements:
bust 45", center back neck to
welt 27", sleeve seam 15"

Gauge/tension:
28 sts and 29½ rows to 4" on
3¼-mm needles over patt

INSTRUCTIONS

BACK

With 2¾-mm needles and Rainforest cast on 158 sts.
Work 2¼" in st st, ending with a P row.
Change to 3¼-mm needles and work picot edge as
foll: K1 (yfwd K2 tog) to end of row.
Next row: P.
Work Chart B from Row 1 to Row 20.
Work Chart A from Row 1 to Row 100 twice.
Shape shoulders: bind off/cast off 54 sts at beg of
next 2 rows.
Bind off/cast off rem 50 sts.

LEFT FRONT

With 2¾-mm needles and Rainforest cast on 63 sts.
Work 2¼" st st, ending with a P row.
Change to 3¼-mm needles and work a picot edge as
for Back.
Next row: P.
Work Chart B from Row 1 to Row 20.
Work Chart A from Row 1 to Row 100 once, then
from Row 1 to Row 65.

MATERIALS

- **3 x 25 g Oatmeal Donegal lambswool tweed**
- **25 g Pickle Donegal lambs-wool tweed**
- **50 g Plum fine cotton chenille**
- **50 g Catkin fine cotton chenille**
- **50 g Ruby fine cotton chenille**
- **50 g Yellow/green DDK**
- **5 x 25 g Rainforest Donegal lambswool tweed**
- **50 g Privet fine cotton chenille**
- **10 x 25 g Cinnamon Donegal lambswool tweed**
- **1 pair 2¾-mm (US 2, UK 12) needles**
- **1 pair 3¼-mm (US 3, UK 10) needles**

Shape neck: keeping continuity of patt dec 1 st at neck edge on next row and foll 5 alt rows, then 1 st at neck edge of foll 4th rows 3 times (54 sts).
Cont without further shaping until Front matches Back to shoulder.
Bind off/cast off.

RIGHT FRONT

Work as for Left Front, reversing all shapings.

SLEEVES

With 2¾-mm needles and Rainforest cast on 126 sts.
Work 2¼" in st st, ending with a P row.
Change to 3¼-mm needles and work a picot edge as for Back.
Next row: P.
Work Chart B from Row 1 to Row 20.
Work Chart A from bottom to top once.
Bind off/cast off in Cinnamon.

LEFT FRONT BAND

With 3¼-mm needles and Rainforest and RS facing, pick up and K 8 sts for every 10 rows down Left Front edge, starting at beg of neck shaping and ending at picot row.
Next row: P.
Foll Chart B for 20 rows, working from Row 20 down to Row 1, and **at the same time, shape neck** by binding-off/casting-off 2 sts at beg of Row 19 and foll 2 alt rows, then dec 1 st at beg of foll 4 alt rows (180 sts).
Change to Rainforest and P 1 row.
Next row: make a picot edge as for Back.
Change to 2¾-mm needles and work 2¼" in st st beg with a P row, and **at the same time, shape neck edge** of facing to correspond to that of Front Band.
Bind off/cast off loosely.

RIGHT FRONT BAND

Work as for Left Front Band, reversing all shapings.

COLLAR

Join shoulder seams.
With 3¼-mm needles and Rainforest and RS facing, pick up and K 41 sts up right side front neck starting at picot edge, 44 sts across back neck, and 41 sts down left side front neck, ending at picot row (126 sts).
Next row: P.
Work Chart B from Row 1 to Row 20.
Next row: using Rainforest work a Picot edge as for Back.
Change to 2¾-mm needles and work 2¼" in st st, starting with a P row.
Bind off/cast off loosely.

FRONT COLLAR EDGINGS

With 2¾-mm needles and Rainforest and RS facing, pick up and K 17 sts along front edge of collar.
Next row: P.
Work a picot edge as for Back.
Work 2¼" st st.
Bind off/cast off.
Work other side to match.

MAKING UP

Tidy loose ends back into their own colors. Position top of Sleeve so that center is at shoulder seam and sew in place. Join Sleeve and side seams. Turn all facings to inside and sew into place with collar facing overlapping front collar edging. Press lightly with a warm iron over a damp cloth.

Ash Kimono: Chart A

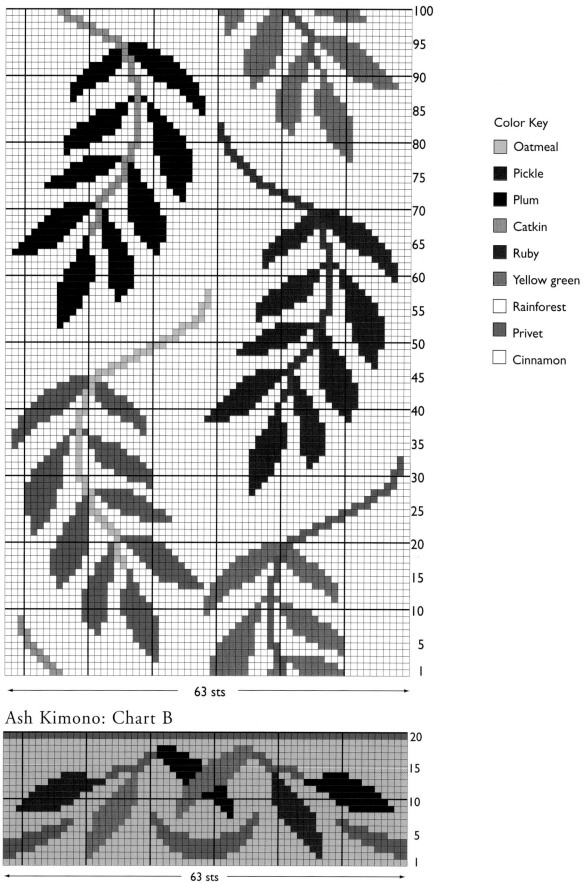

100
95
90
85
80
75
70
65
60
55
50
45
40
35
30
25
20
15
10
5
1

← 63 sts →

Color Key

- ▭ Oatmeal
- ■ Pickle
- ■ Plum
- ▦ Catkin
- ■ Ruby
- ▦ Yellow green
- □ Rainforest
- ▦ Privet
- □ Cinnamon

Ash Kimono: Chart B

20
15
10
5
1

← 63 sts →

Leafy Waistcoat

Actual measurements:
bust 38", center back neck to welt 20"

Gauge/tension:
31 sts and 33½ rows to 4" over patt
on 3¼-mm needles

MATERIALS

FOR MARRAM COLORWAY

- 25 g Bark Donegal lambswool tweed
- 25 g Bay Donegal lambswool tweed
- 25 g Cinnamon Donegal lambswool tweed
- 25 g Bramble Donegal lambswool tweed
- 50 g Robin fine cotton chenille
- 7 x 25 g Marram Donegal lambswool tweed
- 1 pair 2¾-mm (US 2, UK 12) needles
- 1 pair 3¼-mm (US 3, UK 10) needles
- cable needle
- 5 buttons

FOR OATMEAL COLORWAY

- 25 g Rainforest Donegal lambswool tweed
- 50 g Ruby fine cotton chenille
- 25 g Bay Donegal lambswool tweed
- 25 g Cinnamon Donegal lambswool tweed
- 25 g Leaf Donegal lambswool tweed
- 25 g Pickle Donegal lambswool twead
- 7 x 25 g Oatmeal Donegal lambswool tweed

INSTRUCTIONS
Instructions are for both colorways.

BACK

With 2¾-mm needles and Marram/Oatmeal cast on 152 sts.
Work 1½" in K1 P1 twisted rib.
Change to 3¼-mm needles and cont in K1 P1 twisted rib until work measures 10" from cast-on edge.
Armhole shaping: bind off/cast off 4 sts at beg of next 2 rows.
Then K2 tog at each end of every row until 102 sts rem.
Cont straight until armhole measures 9".
Shoulder shaping: Bind off/cast off 9 sts at beg of next 6 rows.
Bind off/cast off rem 48 sts in rib.

LEFT FRONT

With 3¼-mm needles and Marram/Oatmeal cast on 2 sts.
Row 1: K2.
Row 2: m1 P2 m1.

Row 3: m1 K4 m1.
Row 4: m1 K1 P4 K1 m1.
Row 5: m1 P2 K4 P2 m1.
Row 6: m1 P1 K2 P4 K2 P1 m1.
Row 7: m1 K2 P2 C4B P2 K2 m1.
Row 8: m1 P3 K2 P4 K2 P3 m1.

Now foll chart from bottom to top starting at Row 1, placing cable as set, and **at the same time,** cont to inc at both ends of every row until there are 70 sts, taking inc sts into patt as you go.

Keeping continuity of patt work straight until work measures 13" from 2 cast-on sts ending with a K row.

Shape neck: with WS facing and keeping continuity of patt dec 1 st at beg of next row.

Work 2 rows.

Armhole shaping: with RS facing and keeping continuity of patt bind off/cast off 7 sts, work to last 2 sts, K2 tog.

Cont dec 1 st at armhole edge on next 18 rows, and **at the same time,** dec 1 st at neck edge on every 3rd row (37 sts).

Cont straight at armhole edge, but cont to dec at neck edge on every 3rd row until 24 sts rem.

Work straight until armhole measures 9" ending with a P row.

Shoulder shaping: with RS facing and keeping continuity of patt bind off/cast off 8 sts on next 3 alt rows.

RIGHT FRONT

Work as for Left Front, reversing all shapings.

BORDER

With 2¾-mm needles and Marram/Oatmeal cast on 6 sts.

Work cable patt as foll:

Row 1: K4 P2.
Row 2: K2 P4.
Row 3: C4B P2.
Row 4: P4 K2.

Rep Row 1 to Row 4 until work measures 6".

Shape point: *keeping continuity of cable patt work 4 sts turn, work 4 sts turn, work 2 sts, turn work 2 sts, turn work across all 6 sts.

Next row: work across all 6 sts.

Next row: work 2 sts, turn work 2 sts, turn work 4 sts, turn work 4 sts, turn work across all 6 sts.*

Cont in cable patt until work measures 6½" from start of point shaping.

Next row, make buttonhole: with RS facing P2, bind off/cast off 2, K2.

Cast on 2 sts over the bound-of/cast-off sts in previous row.

Cont to rep Row 1 to Row 4 of the cable patt, and **at the same time,** work 4 more buttonholes at 2" intervals.

Cont straight until border is long enough to fit up Right Front, across back of neck, and down Left Front to end at Left Front point when slightly stretched. Then work point shaping instructions from * to *.

Bind off/cast off.

ARMHOLE BORDERS (MAKE TWO)

With 2¾-mm needles and Marram/Oatmeal cast on 6 sts.

Work cable patt for 20".

Bind off/cast off.

MAKING UP

Tidy loose ends back into their own colors. Press Fronts lightly with a warm iron over a damp cloth, omitting cable. Join shoulder seams. Sew Border in place from right side front, along lower edge, up front, around back of neck, and back to left side front. Join side seams. Join each Armhole Border into a circle and set into armhole. Sew on buttons to match buttonholes. Press seams with a warm iron over a damp cloth being careful not to press rib or cables.

Leafy Waistcoat on Marram

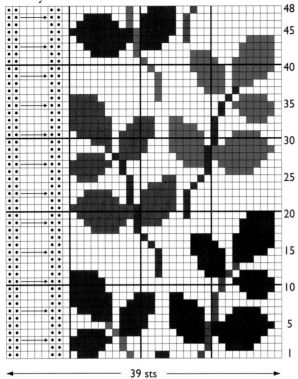

39 sts

Color Key

■ Bark

■ Bay

■ Cinnamon

■ Bramble

■ Robin

□ Marram

● P on K row, K on P row

⊢———▶ Twist cable to the right

Leafy Waistcoat on Oatmeal

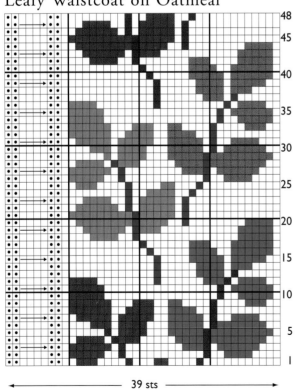

39 sts

Color Key

■ Rainforest

■ Ruby

■ Bay

■ Cinnamon

■ Leaf

■ Pickle

□ Oatmeal

● P on K row, K on P row

⊢———▶ Twist cable to right

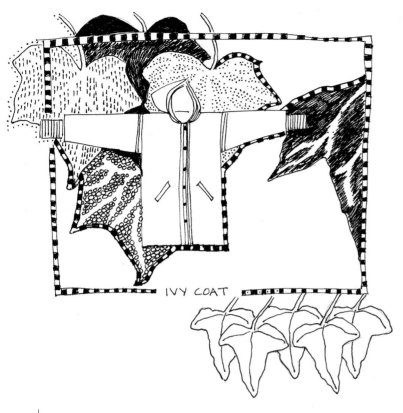

IVY COAT

Ivy Coat with Hood

Actual measurements:
bust 60", center back neck to
welt 31", sleeve seam 19"

Gauge/tension:
24 sts and 26 rows to 4" on
4-mm needles over patt

MATERIALS

- **50 g Crocus fine cotton chenille**
- **25 g Cinnamon Donegal lambswool tweed**
- **50 g Pink DDK**
- **50 g Mallard DK tweed**
- **50 g Blue mint silken tweed**
- **50 g Hare DK tweed**
- **50 g Ruby fine cotton chenille**
- **50 g Skye DK tweed**
- **50 g Forest silken tweed**
- **50 g Damson silken tweed**
- **50 g Copper silken tweed**
- **15 x 50 g Peat DK tweed**
- **1 pair 3¼-mm (US 3, UK 10) needles**
- **1 pair 3¾-mm (US 5, UK 9) needles**
- **1 pair 4-mm (US 6, UK 8) needles**
- **6 buttons**

INSTRUCTIONS

BACK

With 3¾-mm needles and Peat cast on 180 sts.
Work 1" st st, ending with a P row.

Next row: work a picot edge: K1 (yfwd K2 tog) to end.

Work a further 1" st st, starting with a P row.
Change to 4-mm needles and follow chart from bottom to top once, then from Row 22 to Row 51 (on second working of chart the even rows become K rows, read from right to left, and the odd rows become P rows, read from left to right).

Row 52, armhole shaping: second working of chart (RS): keeping continuity of pattern bind off/cast off 9 sts at beg of next 2 rows.

Cont straight to end of chart.

Next row: P in Peat.

Shoulder shaping: working in Peat in K1 P1 twisted rib, bind off/cast off 20 sts at beg of next 6 rows.
Bind off/cast off rem 42 sts in rib.

LEFT FRONT

With 3¾-mm needles and Peat cast on 86 sts.
Work 1" st st, then picot edge as for Back, then 1"
st st.
Change to 4-mm needles and foll chart to Row 70.
Row 71, introduce pocket: keeping continuity of patt
K 20 sts, turn, leaving rem 66 sts on a spare needle.
Work on these 20 sts for 29 more rows, inc 1 st at
left edge on every row, so that the pocket slit slopes
from right to left.
Return to the 66 sts on spare needle and rep Rows 71
to 100, and **at the same time,** dec 1 st at right edge
on every row.
Row 101: patt all 86 sts.
Cont in patt as for Back to Row 51 of second work-
ing of chart.
Row 52, armhole shaping: second working of chart
(RS): bind off/cast off 9 sts at beg of next row.
Cont straight up to and including Row 90.
Row 91, neck shaping: bind off/cast off 6 sts, patt to
end.
Dec 1 st at neck edge on every foll 3rd row 6 times
and then next 5 alt rows (60 sts).
Work straight to end of chart.
Next row: P in Peat.
Shoulder shaping: working in Peat only in K1 P1
twisted rib, bind off/cast off 20 sts at beg of next 3
alt rows in rib.

RIGHT FRONT

Work as for Left Front, reversing all shapings and
starting chart at st 27.
Start pocket slit 66 sts from center front, making it
slope from left to right by dec on right side and inc
on left side.

SLEEVES

With 3¾-mm needles and Crocus cast on 52 sts.
Work 1 row K1 P1 twisted rib.
Change to Peat and work 4" in K1 P1 twisted rib.
Change to 4-mm needles and work Row 1 to Row
99, and **at the same time,** inc 1 st at both ends of
next and every foll 3rd row until there are 120 sts,
taking extra sts into patt as they occur.

In Peat only P 1 row.
In Peat only work 9 rows K1 P1 twisted rib.
Bind off/cast off loosely in rib.

LEFT FRONT BAND

With 3¾-mm needles and Peat and RS facing, pick up
and K 1 st for each row from neck to fold of picot
edge.
Work 12 rows in K1 P1 twisted rib.
Change to Crocus and work 1 row K1 P1 twisted rib.
Bind off/cast off in rib with Crocus.

RIGHT FRONT BAND

With 3¾-mm needles and Peat and RS facing, pick up
and K 1 st for each row from fold of picot edge to
neck (making sure you have the same number of sts
as for Left Front Band).
Work 5 rows in K1 P1 twisted rib.
Work 6 buttonholes evenly along next row by binding
off/casting off 4 sts for each hole and starting first
hole 6" up from picot edge.
Next row: cast on 4 sts over bound-off/cast-off sts in
previous row.
Work 5 more rows K1 P1 twisted rib.
Change to Crocus and work 1 row K1 P1 twisted rib.
Bind off/cast off in rib with Crocus.

HOOD

With 3¾-mm needles and Crocus, cast on 172 sts.
Work 1 row K1 P1 twisted rib.
Change to Peat and work 12 rows K1 P1 twisted rib.
Change to 4-mm needles and follow chart up to and
including Row 72, and **at the same time,** shape Hood
as foll:
Work straight to Row 8, then dec 1 st at each end of
every 3rd row 6 times, then at each end of next 5 alt
rows. Cont straight to Row 72.
Bind off/cast off with Peat.

Ivy Coat with Hood

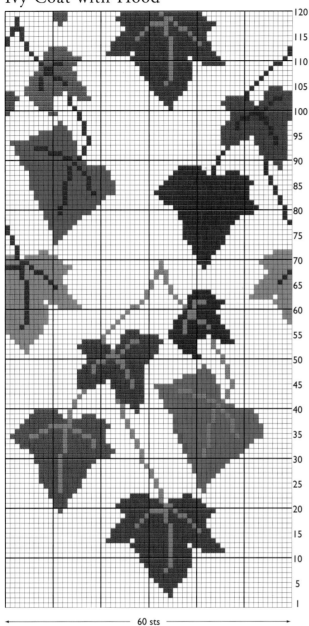

60 sts

Color Key

- ■ Crocus
- ▨ Cinnamon (use double)
- ■ Pink DDK
- ▨ Mallard
- ▨ Blue mint
- ▨ Hare
- ■ Ruby
- ■ Skye
- ▨ Forest
- ▨ Damson
- ■ Copper
- □ Peat

POCKET TOPS

With 3¼-mm needles and Peat and RS facing, pick up and K 1 st for each row up the side of the pocket slit nearest the front opening edge.
Work 9 rows K1 P1 twisted rib.
Change to Crocus and work 1 row K1 P1 twisted rib.
Bind off/cast off in rib with Crocus.

POCKET LININGS

With 4-mm needles and Peat and RS facing, pick up and K 1 st for each row up side of pocket slit nearest side seam.
Work 4" in st st, starting with a P row so that the smooth side of the st st will be touching the hand in the pocket.
Bind off/cast off.

MAKING UP

Tidy loose ends back into their own colors. Join shoulder seams. Sew bound-off/cast-off edge of Sleeve top into armhole, the straight sides at top of Sleeve to form a neat right angle at bound-off/cast-off sts of armhole at Front and Back. Join rest of Sleeve and underarm seam. Join sides of Pocket Tops to main work and sew down Pocket Linings. Fold welts to inside and hem. Attach Hood to neck. Sew on buttons to match buttonholes. Press lightly with a warm iron over a damp cloth.

Dancing Leaves Blouson Jacket

Actual measurements:
bust 47", center back neck to welt 25", sleeve seam 18"

Gauge/tension:
19½ sts and 27 rows to 4" on 4½-mm needles over patt

INSTRUCTIONS

BACK

With 3¾-mm needles and Dolphin cast on 115 sts.
Work 1½" seed st/moss st.
Change to 4½-mm needles and foll chart from bottom to top, then from Row 11 to top, until work measures 16½" from cast-on edge.
Armhole shaping: keeping continuity of patt bind off/cast off 6 sts at beg of next 2 rows.
Cont straight until armhole measures 9".
Shoulder shaping: working in Dolphin in seed st/moss st, bind off/cast off 11 sts at beg of next 6 rows.
Bind off/cast off rem 37 sts.

LEFT FRONT

With 3¾-mm needles and Dolphin cast on 56 sts.
Work 1½" seed st/moss st.
Change to 4½-mm needles and foll chart from bottom up to and including Row 30 on first working of chart.
Row 31, divide for pocket: patt 28 sts, turn and leave rem 28 sts on a holder.

MATERIALS

- 50 g Privet fine cotton chenille
- 100 g Maple cotton chenille
- 100 g Admiral magpie Aran
- 2 x 50 g Wren DK tweed
- 100 g Sienna magpie tweed
- 50 g Plum fine cotton chenille
- 100 g Ember magpie tweed
- 100 g Lush cotton chenille
- 100 g Rose magpie Aran
- 7 x 100 g Dolphin magpie Aran
- 1 pair 3¾-mm (US 5, UK 9) needles
- 1 pair 4½-mm (US 7, UK 7) needles
- 2 stitch holders
- 9 buttons

Work each side of pocket separately as foll:
Work 26 rows in patt (on reaching Row 50 return to Row 11) and leave these sts on a holder.
Return to rem 28 sts, rejoin yarns and work to match first side of pocket.
Next row (Row 18 on chart): patt across all 56 sts.
Cont without further shaping up to top of chart and then from Row 11 until work measures same as Back to armhole shaping, ending with a P row.
Armhole shaping: keeping continuity of patt bind off/cast off 6 sts at beg of row.
Cont straight until work measures 22" from cast-on edge, ending with a K row.
Neck shaping: bind off/cast off 4 sts at beg of row, patt to end.
Work 1 row.
K2 tog at neck edge on next 13 rows.
Cont without further shaping until armhole measures same as Back.
Shoulder shaping: working in Dolphin in seed st/moss st bind off/cast off 11 sts at beg of next 3 alt rows.

RIGHT FRONT

The Right Front is a mirror image of the Left Front. Work as for Left Front, reversing all shapings and starting Row 1 of chart with a P row to reverse patt.

SLEEVES

With 3¾-mm needles and Dolphin cast on 39 sts.
Work 2" in seed st/moss st.
Change to 4½-mm needles and foll chart from bottom to top, and then from Row 11 to top, starting at st 14 on Row 1, and **at the same time,** inc 1 st at both ends of the next and every foll 4th row until there are 85 sts, taking extra sts into patt as they occur.
Cont straight until work measures 18" from cast-on edge.
Change to Dolphin and work 1" seed st/moss st.
Bind off/cast off loosely in Dolphin.

LEFT FRONT BAND

With 4½-mm needles and Dolphin and RS facing, pick up and K 110 sts evenly along Left Front from start of neck shaping to cast-on edge.
Work 1" seed st/moss st.
Bind off/cast off loosely.

RIGHT FRONT BAND

With 3-mm needles and Dolphin and RS facing, pick up and K 110 sts evenly along Right Front from cast-on edge to start of neck shaping.
Work ½" seed st/moss st.
Next row: work 8 buttonholes evenly spaced between neck and welt, binding off/casting off 3 sts for each hole.
Next row: cast on 3 sts over the bound-off/cast-off sts in previous row.
Cont in seed st/moss st until band measures 1".
Bind off/cast off.

COLLAR

Join shoulder seams.
With 3¾-mm needles and Plum (use double) and with WS facing, starting at Right Front Band pick up and K 6 sts (from band), 34 sts up Right Front, 29 sts across Back, 34 sts down Left Front, and 6 sts from band (109 sts).
Work in seed st/moss st for 19 rows, placing a buttonhole in Row 16 (3 sts in from right edge) and binding off/casting off 3 sts for hole.
Row 17: cast on 3 sts over the bound-off/cast-off sts in previous row.
Bind off/cast off firmly.

POCKET LININGS

With 4½-mm needles and Dolphin and RS facing, pick up and K 26 sts evenly along side edge of pocket slit nearest to side edge of Front.
Work 10" in st st, beg with a P row.
Bind off/cast off.

Dancing Leaves Blouson Jacket

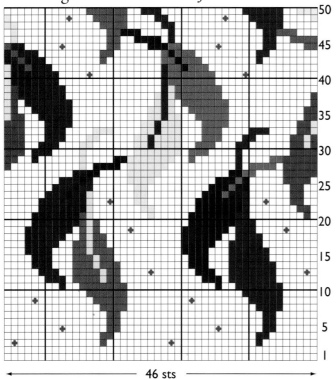

46 sts

Color Key

■ Privet

■ Maple

■ Admiral

☐ Wren (use double)

■ Sienna

■ Plum

■ Ember

■ Lush

■ Rose

☐ Dolphin

✿ Make bobble (see p. 169)

Follow chart from bottom to top once,
then repeat chart from row 11 to top.

MAKING UP

Tidy loose ends back into their own colors. Sew
bound-off/cast-off edge of Sleeve top into armhole,
the straight sides at top of Sleeve to form a neat right
angle at bound-off/cast-off sts of armhole at Front
and Back. Join rest of Sleeve and underarm seams.
Sew bound-off/cast-off edge of Pocket Linings to edge
of pocket slit nearest center front. Oversew sides of
Pocket Linings. Sew on buttons to match buttonholes.
Press lightly with a warm iron over a damp cloth.

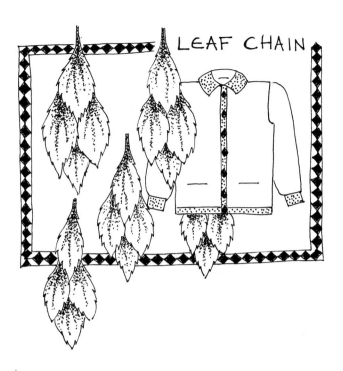

LEAF CHAIN

Leaf Chain Jacket

Actual measurements:
bust 52", center back neck to
welt 29", sleeve seam 15"

Gauge/tension:
25 sts and 28 rows to 4" on
3¾-mm needles over patt

INSTRUCTIONS

BACK

With 3¼-mm needles and Penguin cast on 150 sts.
Work 2" K1 P1 twisted rib.
Change to 3¾-mm needles and foll chart from bottom to top once and then from Row 13 to top until work measures 18½" from cast-on edge.
Armhole shaping: keeping continuity of patt bind off/cast off 5 sts at beg of next 2 rows.
Then dec 1 st at both ends of next 5 rows, then at both ends of foll 9 alt rows (112 sts).
Cont straight until armhole measures 9", ending with a P row.
Shoulder shaping: keeping continuity of patt bind off/cast off 12 sts at beg of next 6 rows.
Bind off/cast off rem 40 sts.

LEFT FRONT

With 3¼-mm needles and Penguin cast on 75 sts.
Work 2" K1 P1 twisted rib.
Change to 3¾-mm needles and foll chart for 4", ending with a P row.

MATERIALS

- **2 x 25 g Bramble Donegal lambswool tweed**
- **50 g Skye DK tweed**
- **2 x 50 g Rose pink DDK**
- **50 g Ruby fine cotton chenille**
- **2 x 50 g Toad silken tweed**
- **2 x 50 g Forest silken tweed**
- **50 g Catkin fine cotton chenille**
- **5 x 25 g Cinnamon Donegal lambswool tweed**
- **9 x 50 g Penguin DK tweed**
- **1 pair 3¼-mm (US 3, UK 10) needles**
- **1 pair 3¾-mm (US 5, UK 9) needles**
- **8 buttons**

Introduce pocket: patt 51 sts, turn, P27, turn. Working on these 27 sts, using Penguin only, complete 8" st st, starting and ending with a K row. Return to 24 sts on left side and patt to end. Then patt all 75 sts until work measures 18½" from cast-on edge, ending with a P row.

Armhole shaping: keeping continuity of patt bind off/cast off 5 sts at beg of next row.

Then dec 1 st at armhole edge on next 5 rows, then on foll 9 alt rows (56 sts).

Cont straight until work measures 23" from cast-on edge, ending with a K row.

Neck shaping: keeping continuity of patt bind off/cast off 3 sts at beg of next row, then 2 sts twice on alt rows, then 1 st at beg of every foll alt row until 36 sts rem.

Cont straight until work matches Back to shoulder shaping, ending with a P row.

Shoulder shaping: keeping continuity of patt bind off/cast off 12 sts at beg of next 3 alt rows.

RIGHT FRONT

Work as for Left Front, reversing all shapings and starting chart at st 16 on Row 1.

SLEEVES

With 3¼-mm needles and Penguin cast on 60 sts. Work 2½" K1 P1 twisted rib.

Change to 3¾-mm needles and foll chart from bottom to top once and then from Row 13, and **at the same time,** inc 1 st at each end of next row and every foll 4th row until there are 100 sts, taking extra sts into patt as they occur.

Cont straight until sleeve measures 14½" from cast-on edge.

Shape top: keeping continuity of patt bind off/cast off 5 sts at beg of next 2 rows.

Then dec 1 st at both ends of next 5 rows, then at both ends of foll 18 alt rows (44 sts).

Then bind off/cast off 2 sts at beg of next 2 rows, then 3 sts at beg of next 2 rows and then 4 sts at beg of next 2 rows.

Bind off/cast off rem 26 sts.

LEFT FRONT BAND

With 3¼-mm needles and Penguin, pick up and K 7 sts for each 8 rows from neck to welt.

Work 1" K1 P1 twisted rib.

Bind off/cast off in rib.

Leaf Chain Jacket

Color Key

- ⬛ Bramble (use double)
- ⬛ Skye
- ⬜ Rose pink
- ⬛ Ruby
- ⬛ Toad
- ⬛ Forest
- ⬜ Catkin
- ⬛ Cinnamon (use double)
- ⬜ Penguin

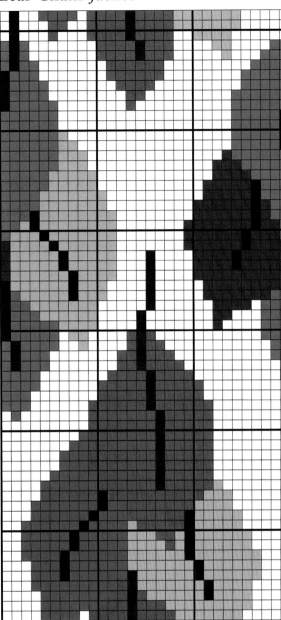

← 30 sts →

RIGHT FRONT BAND

Work as for Left Band, but work 8 buttonholes evenly spaced along band in Row 3, starting first buttonhole after 4 sts have been worked and last hole 4 sts from end. Bind off/cast off 3 sts for each hole; in next row cast on 3 sts over the bound-off/cast-off sts. Cont to match Left Front Band.

COLLAR

With 3¼-mm needles and Ruby cast on 41 sts and, working in seed st/moss st throughout, work 1 row, then cast on 6 sts at beg of next 10 rows (101 sts). Cont on these sts for 3".
Bind off/cast off loosely.

MAKING UP

Tidy loose ends back into their own colors. Join shoulder seams and side seams. Join Sleeve seams. Set and sew Sleeves into armhole. Sew Collar to neck. Oversew sides of Pocket Linings. Sew buttons on to match buttonholes. Press lightly with a warm iron over a damp cloth.

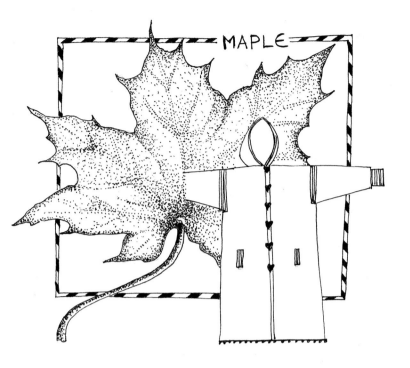

Maple Coat with Hood

Actual measurements:
bust 62", center back neck to
welt 31", sleeve seam 17"

Gauge/tension:
22 sts and 27½ rows to 4" on
4-mm needles over patt

INSTRUCTIONS

BACK

With 3¾-mm needles and Olive cast on 170 sts.
Work 8 rows st st.
Next row: work a picot edge as foll: K1 (yfwd K2 tog) to end of row.
P next row.
Change to 4-mm needles and foll chart from bottom to top once then from Row 7 to top until work measures 21" from picot edge line.
Armhole shaping: bind off/cast off 9 sts at beg of next 2 rows.
Cont straight until armhole measures 10".
In Olive only, work 1 row st st.
Shoulder shaping: work K1 P1 twisted rib in stripe sequence as foll:
Row 1: Yellow/green.
Row 2: Catkin (use single).
Row 3: Olive.
Bind off/cast off 18 sts at beg of next 4 rows and 19 sts at beg of next 2 rows.
Bind off/cast off rem 42 sts.

MATERIALS

- 100 g Pale brown DK chenille, Colinette Yarns
- 2 x 50 g Catkin fine cotton chenille
- 50 g Peat DK tweed
- 2 x 50 g Yellow/green DDK
- 3 x 50 g Olive DDK
- 100 g Claret DK chenille, Colinette Yarns
- 100 g Ochre DK chenille, Colinette Yarns
- 100 g Fire random DK chenille, Colinette Yarns
- 100 g Chestnut DK chenille, Colinette Yarns
- 12 x 50 g Hare DK tweed
- 1 pair 3¼-mm (US 3, UK 10) needles
- 1 pair 3¾-mm (US 5, UK 9) needles
- 1 pair 4-mm (US 6, UK 8) needles
- 4 buttons

LEFT FRONT

With 3¾-mm needles and Olive cast on 85 sts.
Work 8 rows st st, then work a picot edge as for Back.
P next row.
Change to 4-mm needles and foll chart from bottom up to and including Row 70.
Pocket slit: work pocket over next 30 rows as foll:
Next row: work first 30 sts, turn, leaving rem sts on a spare needle.
Work next 29 rows in patt on these 30 sts.
Return to sts on spare needle and work 30 rows in patt.
Now slip both sets of sts onto one needle and continue in patt until Front measures same as Back to armhole, ending with a WS row.
Armhole shaping: bind off/cast off 9 sts at beg of next row.
Cont straight until work measures 25" from picot edge line, ending with a RS row.
Neck shaping: bind off/cast off 8 sts, patt to end.
Then dec 1 st at neck edge on every 3rd row 6 times, then next 4 alt rows, and then next 3 rows (55 sts).
Cont straight until Front measures same as Back.
With Olive only and WS facing, P 1 row.
Shoulder shaping: with RS facing and in K1 P1 twisted rib in stripe sequence, bind off/cast off 18 sts at beg of next 2 alt rows and 19 sts at beg of next alt row.

RIGHT FRONT

Work as for Left Front, reversing all shapings and starting chart at st 1 with a P row to produce a mirror image. Work pocket slit 56 sts from center front.

SLEEVES

With 3¾-mm needles and Olive cast on 52 sts.
Work 4" K1 P1 twisted rib in stripe sequence.
Change to 4-mm needles and foll chart from bottom to top once, starting at st 18 on Row 1, and **at the same time,** inc 1 st at both ends of next and every foll 3rd row until there are 112 sts, taking extra sts into patt as they occur.
With Olive only P 1 row.
Work 9 rows K1 P1 twisted rib in stripe sequence.
Bind off/cast off loosely in rib in Olive.

LEFT FRONT BAND

With 3¾-mm needles and Olive and RS facing, pick up and K 1 st for each row from neck to picot edge line.
Work 12 rows in K1 P1 twisted rib in stripe sequence.
Bind off/cast off in rib in Olive.

RIGHT FRONT BAND

With 3¾-mm needles and Olive and RS facing, pick up and K 1 st for each row from picot edge line to neck (making sure you have the same number of sts as for Left Front Band).
Work 5 rows in K1 P1 twisted rib in stripe sequence.
Next row (still in stripe sequence): work 4 buttonholes evenly along row, binding off/casting off 5 sts for each hole, starting first hole 6" from picot edge and last hole ending 1" from start of neck shaping.
Next row: cast on 5 sts over bound-off/cast-off sts in previous row.
Work 5 more rows K1 P1 twisted rib in stripe sequence.
Bind off/cast off in rib in Olive.

HOOD

With 3¼-mm needles and Olive, cast on 172 sts.
Work 12 rows K1 P1 twisted rib in stripe sequence.
Change to 4-mm needles and foll chart from bottom
up to and including Row 72, and **at the same time,**
shape hood as foll:
Work straight to Row 8, then dec 1 st at each end of
every 3rd row 6 times, then at each end of next 5 alt
rows. Cont straight to Row 72.
Bind off/cast off.

POCKET TOPS

With 3¼-mm needles and Olive and RS facing, pick
up and K 33 sts up side of pocket slit nearest front
opening edge.
Work 7 rows K1 P1 twisted rib in stripe sequence.
Bind off/cast off in Olive.

POCKET LININGS

With 3¼-mm needles and Olive and RS facing, pick
up and K 30 sts up side of pocket slit nearest side
seam.
Work 4" st st.
Bind off/cast off.

MAKING UP

Tidy loose ends back into their own colors. Join
shoulder seams. Sew bound-off/cast-off edge of Sleeve
top into armhole, the straight sides at top of Sleeve to
form a neat right angle at bound-off/cast-off sts of
armhole at Front and Back. Join rest of Sleeve and
underarm seams. Fold lower edge at picot line to
inside and hem in place. Seam back of Hood. Attach
Hood around neck. Join sides of Pocket Tops to main
work. Sew down Pocket Linings. Sew on buttons to
match buttonholes. Press lightly with a warm iron
over a damp cloth.

Maple Coat with Hood

85 sts

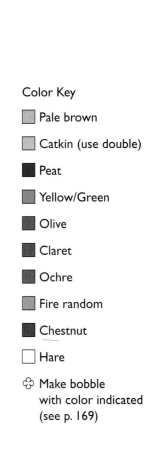

Color Key

■ Pale brown

■ Catkin (use double)

■ Peat

■ Yellow/Green

■ Olive

■ Claret

■ Ochre

■ Fire random

■ Chestnut

□ Hare

⚘ Make bobble
with color indicated
(see p. 169)

Meadow Flowers

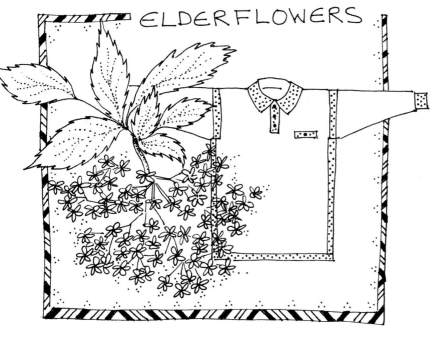

Elderflowers Shirt

Actual measurements:
bust 52", center neck to welt 30",
sleeve seam 16"

Gauge/tension:
22 sts and 28 rows to 4" on 3¾-mm
needles over patt

INSTRUCTIONS

BACK

With 2¾-mm needles and Frost cast on 142 sts.
Work 6 rows seed st/moss st.
Change to 3¾-mm needles and work 1st row as foll:
5 sts seed st/moss st, Row 1 of chart 3 times, 5 sts
seed st/moss st.
Cont as set, foll chart from bottom to top until work
measures 29".
Shoulder shaping: keeping continuity of patt bind
off/cast off 21 sts at beg of next 2 rows and 16 sts at
beg of next 4 rows.
Bind off/cast off rem 36 sts.

FRONT

Make one pocket lining as foll: with 3¾-mm needles
and Frost cast on 21 sts. Work 4½" st st.
Place sts onto a stitch holder.
Then work as for Back until work measures 21" from
cast-on edge, ending with a P row.
Divide for placket and pocket: keeping continuity of
patt and RS facing, work 26 sts, place next 21 sts
onto a stitch holder and in their place work across

MATERIALS

- **50 g Copper silken tweed**
- **50 g Grape silken tweed**
- **25 g Tan lightweight DK**
- **25 g Pale yellow lightweight DK**
- **3 x 50 g Ecru fine cotton chenille**
- **2 x 50 g Parched fine cotton chenille**
- **100 g Lily chunky cotton chenille**
- **100 g Forest chunky cotton chenille**
- **12 x 50 g Frost silken tweed**
- **1 pair 2¾-mm (US 2, UK 12) needles**
- **1 pair 3¾-mm (US 5, UK 9) needles**
- **3 stitch holders**
- **3 buttons**

Elderflowers Shirt

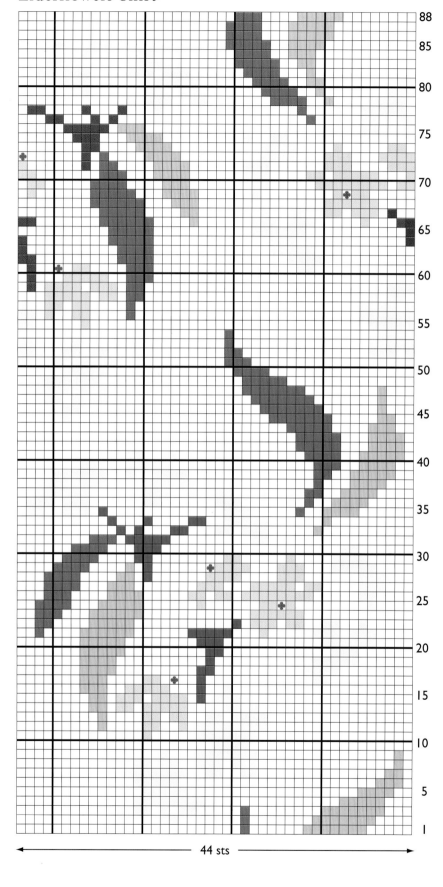

88
85
80
75
70
65
60
55
50
45
40
35
30
25
20
15
10
5
1

← 44 sts →

Color Key

☐ Frost

■ Copper

▨ Grape

■ Tan

☐ Pale yellow

☐ Ecru

▨ Parched

▨ Lily

■ Forest

✿ Make bobble with single
strand of color indicated
(see p. 169)

- Parched flowers have
  Tan bobbles
- Ecru flowers have Pale yellow
  bobbles
- Lily flowers have Ecru bobbles
  (use single yarn)

21 sts of pocket lining, patt across next 21 sts, and turn (68 sts).

Place rem 74 sts onto a stitch holder.

Working on the 68 sts of left front, cont straight until work measures 25½", ending with a K row.

Neck shaping: keeping continuity of patt and WS facing, dec 1 st at neck edge on foll 15 rows (53 sts). Cont straight until Front measures same as Back to shoulder shaping, ending with a P row.

Shoulder shaping: keeping continuity of patt bind off/cast off 21 sts at beg of next row and 16 sts at beg of next 2 alt rows.

Return to 74 sts on stitch holder.

With RS facing, place first 6 sts onto a stitch holder. Working on rem 68 sts work right front to match left front, omitting pocket and reversing all shapings.

SLEEVES

With 2¾-mm needles and Frost cast on 50 sts.

Work 2½" seed st/moss st.

Change to 3¾-mm needles and foll chart from bottom to top once, starting chart at st 41 on Row 1, and **at the same time,** inc 1 st at both ends of Row 1 and every foll 3rd row until there are 104 sts, taking inc sts into patt as they occur.

Cont straight until work measures 16" from cast-on edge.

Bind off/cast off loosely.

PLACKET

Place 6 sts of placket onto a 2¾-mm needle and work 4¼" seed st/moss st in Frost.

Bind off/cast off in seed st/moss st.

With 2¾-mm needles and Frost and RS facing, pick up and K 26 sts along right side of placket (so that the piece just knitted will be underneath this next piece).

Work 1 row in seed st/moss st.

Next row: work 3 buttonholes evenly spaced along placket, casting off 3 sts for each hole.

Next row: cast on 3 sts over the bound-off/cast-off sts in previous row.

Cont in seed st/moss st until 6 rows have been completed in all.

Bind off/cast off in seed st/moss st.

COLLAR

With 2¾-mm needles and Frost cast on 109 sts.

Work 2½" seed st/moss st.

Shape collar:

Row 1: patt 9, turn, patt to end.

Row 2: patt 6, turn, patt to end.

Row 3: patt 3, turn, patt to end.

Row 4: patt across all sts.

Rep Row 1 to Row 3.

Bind off/cast off in seed st/moss st.

POCKET TOP

With 2¾-mm needles and Frost and RS facing, work 6 rows seed st/moss st on 21 sts of pocket.

Bind off/cast off in seed st/moss st.

MAKING UP

Tidy loose ends back into their own colors. Join shoulder seams. Set Sleeve so that center of Sleeve lines up with shoulder seam, then sew in place. Join Sleeve seams and then side seams, leaving bottom 8" loose to form a side slit. Sew Placket to Front and sew on buttons to match buttonholes. With WS tog sew Collar to neck, starting one edge halfway across Placket Top and finishing the other edge halfway across Placket Top. Sew down sides of Pocket Top and Lining. Press lightly with a warm iron over a damp cloth.

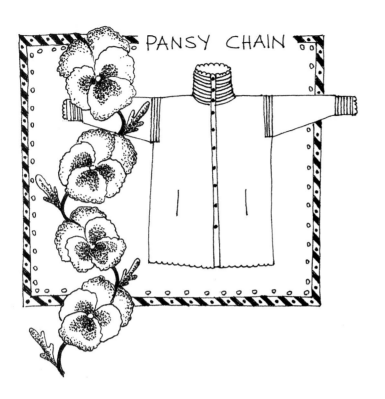

Pansy Chain Coat

Actual measurements:
bust 48", center back neck to welt
30", sleeve seam 16"

Gauge/tension:
23 sts and 27½ rows to 4" on 4-mm
needles over patt

MATERIALS

- **25 g Yellow lightweight DK**
- **50 g Privet fine cotton chenille**
- **50 g Catkin fine cotton chenille**
- **25 g Tan lightweight DK**
- **2 x 50 g Mahogany DDK**
- **3 x 25 g Orange/red lightweight DK**
- **50 g Robin fine cotton chenille**
- **25 g Orange lightweight DK**
- **50 g Copper silken tweed**
- **3 x 50 g Plum fine cotton chenille**
- **25 g Deep pink lightweight DK**
- **50 g Crocus fine cotton chenille**
- **50 g Milkshake fine cotton chenille**
- **2 x 50 g Mid pink DDK**
- **25 g Pale rose pink lightweight DK**
- **11 x 50 g Seal DK tweed**
- **1 pair 3¾-mm (US 5, UK 9) needles**
- **1 pair 4-mm (US 6, UK 8) needles**
- **10 buttons**

INSTRUCTIONS

BACK

With 4-mm needles and Seal cast on 140 sts.
Work 1" st st, ending with a P row.
Next row: work a picot edge: K1 (yfwd K2 tog) to
last st, K1.
P 1 row.
Then follow chart from bottom to top until work
measures 22½" from picot edge line, ending with a
P row.
Armhole shaping: keeping continuity of patt bind
off/cast off 9 sts at beg of next 2 rows (122 sts).
Cont straight until armhole measures 10", ending
with a P row.
Next row: patt 38 sts, turn.
Working on these 38 sts only and keeping continuity
of patt, dec 1 st at neck edge on the foll 6 rows.
Next row: bind off/cast off in Seal.
Return to rem sts, rejoin yarn, bind off/cast off 46 sts
and work to end of row in patt.
Then dec 1 st at neck edge on foll 6 rows to match
left side.
Bind off/cast off in Seal.

Pansy Chain Coat

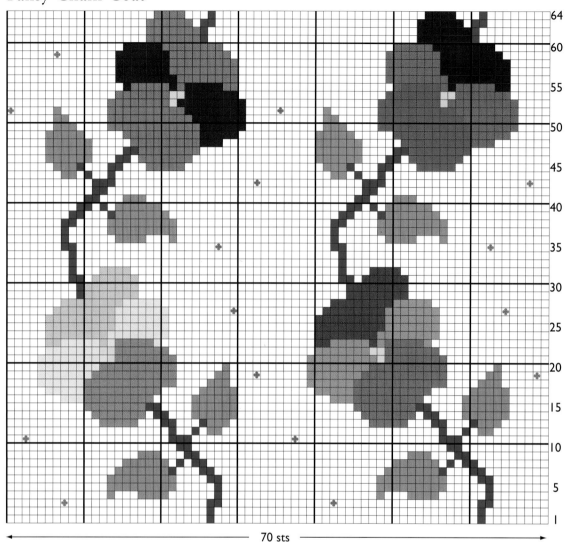

70 sts

Color Key

▢ Yellow		▨ Deep pink	
▨ Privet		▨ Crocus	
▨ Catkin		▨ Milkshake	
▨ Tan		▨ Mid pink	
▧ Mahogany		▢ Pale rose/Pink	
▨ Orange/Red		▢ Seal	
▧ Robin		✤ Make bobble with	
▨ Orange		color indicated	
▨ Copper		(see p. 169)	
▨ Plum			

(see p. 169)

LEFT FRONT

With 4-mm needles and Seal cast on 70 sts.
Work 1" st st, ending with a P row.
Next row: work a picot edge: K1 (yfwd K2 tog) to last st, K1.
P 1 row.
Follow chart from bottom to top once, then up to and including Row 16.
Pocket slit: work first 35 sts, turn, leaving rem sts on a spare needle.
Patt next 29 rows on these sts.
Return to sts on spare needle and patt 30 rows.
Then slip both sets of sts onto one needle and continue as for Back up to armhole shaping, ending with a WS row.

Armhole shaping: keeping continuity of patt and with RS facing, bind off/cast off 9 sts at beg of row. Cont straight up to and including Row 7 of fourth working of chart.

Neck shaping: keeping continuity of patt and WS facing, bind off/cast off 6 sts, patt to end. Then dec 1 st at neck edge of foll 23 rows. Cont straight until Front measures same as Back to shoulder.

Bind off/cast off in Seal.

RIGHT FRONT

Work as for Left Front, reversing all shapings.

SLEEVES

With 3¾-mm needles and Plum chenille cast on 58 sts.

Work 2¼" st st, ending with a P row.

Next row: work a picot edge: K1 (yfwd K2 tog) to last st, K1.

P 1 row.

Change to K1 P1 twisted rib in the foll stripe sequence for 24 rows:

Row 1: Mid pink.

Row 2: Orange/red.

Row 3: Mahogany.

Change to 4-mm needles and Seal.

Next row: K, inc 12 sts evenly across row (70 sts).

P 1 row.

Then foll chart from bottom to top 1½ times (96 rows), and **at the same time,** inc 1 st at both ends of every foll 4th row until there are 116 sts, taking extra sts into patt as they occur.

Work 9 rows K1 P1 twisted rib in stripe sequence. Bind off/cast off in rib.

COLLAR

Join shoulder seams.

With 3¾-mm needles and Mahogany and RS facing, pick up and K 1 st for each row from right front edge up right neck shaping, across back neck, down left neck shaping to left front edge.

Work 9" in stripe sequence in K1 P1 twisted rib, ending with a WS row.

Change to Plum and K 1 row, then P 1 row.

Next row: work a picot edge: K1 (yfwd K2 tog) to last st, K1.

P 1 row.

Continue in st st until Collar measures 18¼" from picked-up sts.

Bind off/cast off loosely.

LEFT FRONT BAND

With 3¾-mm needles and Mahogany and RS facing, pick up and K 1 st for each row from picot edge on Collar to picot edge at bottom of Left Front.

Work 12 rows in stripe sequence in K1 P1 twisted rib.

Bind off/cast off in twisted rib in Mid pink.

RIGHT FRONT BAND

Work as for Left Band, except make 7 buttonholes along Row 6, starting the first hole 6" from bottom picot edge and last hole ½" from start of neck shaping, and **at the same time,** work 3 buttonholes evenly along collar from neck shaping to picot edge, binding off/casting off 3 sts for each hole.

Row 7: cast on 3 sts over the bound-off/cast-off sts in previous row.

POCKET LININGS

With 3¾-mm needles and Plum, and RS facing, pick up and K 1 st for each row along one of the four pocket edges. Work 4½" st st, starting with a P row. Bind off/cast off.

Rep with each of the other 3 pocket edges.

MAKING UP

Tidy loose ends back into their own colors. Sew bound-off/cast-off edge of Sleeve top into armhole, the straight sides at top of Sleeve to form a neat right angle at bound-off/cast-off sts of armhole at Front and Back. Join rest of Sleeve and side seams. Turn all facings to inside at picot edge and hem into place. Seam edges of Pocket Linings together. Sew on buttons to match buttonholes. Press lightly with a warm iron over a damp cloth.

Cornfield Crew-Neck Sweater

Actual measurements:
bust 42", center back neck to welt 25½", sleeve seam 17½"

Gauge/tension:
28 sts and 30½ rows to 4" on 3¼-mm needles over patt

MATERIALS

- 2 x 25 g Pale green lightweight DK
- 25 g Olive green lightweight DK
- 4 x 25 g Tarragon Donegal lambswool tweed
- 2 x 25 g Pale yellow lightweight DK
- 50 g Crocus fine cotton chenille
- 25 g Bluebell lightweight DK
- 25 g Lilac lightweight DK
- 25 g Light purple lightweight DK
- 2 x 25 g Magenta lightweight DK
- 25 g Pale pink lightweight DK
- 2 x 25 g Mauve lightweight DK
- 50 g Milkshake fine cotton chenille
- 50 g Robin fine cotton chenille
- 10 x 25 g Elderberry Donegal lambswool tweed
- 1 pair 2¾-mm (US 2, UK 12) needles
- 1 pair 3¼-mm (US 3, UK 10) needles
- 2 stitch holders

INSTRUCTIONS

BACK

With 2¾-mm needles and Tarragon cast on 150 sts. Work 17 rows in st st, starting with a K row.
Next row:
K to form a fold line.
Change to 3¼-mm needles and work 14 rows in bi-color rib (carrying yarn not in use on WS of each row) as foll:
Row 1: (P2 Tarragon, K2 Crocus) to last 2 sts, P2 Tarragon.
Row 2: (K2 Tarragon, P2 Crocus) to last 2 sts, K2 Tarragon.
Then foll chart from bottom to top until work measures 16½" from cast-on edge.
Armhole shaping: keeping continuity of patt bind off/cast off 8 sts at beg of next 2 rows.
Cont straight until armhole measures 8½".
Shoulder shaping: keeping continuity of patt bind off/cast off 12 sts at beg of next 6 rows.
Place rem 62 sts onto a stitch holder.

FRONT

Work as for Back, until Front is 24 rows shorter than Back to start of shoulder shaping.

Neck shaping: patt 51 sts, turn, and leave rem sts on a stitch holder.

Bind off/cast off at neck edge on next row and foll alt rows 4 sts once, 3 sts twice, 2 sts once, and 1 st 3 times (36 sts).

Cont straight until Front matches Back to shoulder.

Shoulder shaping: keeping continuity of patt and RS facing bind off/cast off 12 sts at beg of foll 3 alt rows.

With RS facing, rejoin yarn to rem sts, bind off/cast off 32 sts, patt to end.

Complete second side to match first, reversing all shaping.

SLEEVES

With 3¼-mm needles and Tarragon cast on 62 sts.

Work 14 rows in bicolor rib as for Back.

Then foll chart from bottom to top starting at st 45 on Row 1, and **at the same time**, inc 1 st at both ends of next and every foll 4th row until there are 120 sts, taking the extra sts into the patt as they occur, ending with a P row.

Work 5 rows without shaping.

Change to Tarragon and K 1 row.

Then work 9 rows bicolor rib as foll:

Row 1 (WS): (K2 Tarragon, P2 Crocus) to end.

Row 2: (K2 Crocus, P2 Tarragon) to end.

Bind off/cast off in Tarragon.

NECKBAND

Join right shoulder seam.

With 3¼-mm needles and Tarragon and RS facing, pick up and K 1 st for each row down left side of neck, across Front, up right side of neck, and across 62 sts at back neck (making sure that you have a number of sts divisible by 4).

Work 9 rows bicolor rib as for top of Sleeve.

Change to 2¾-mm needles and Tarragon.

With RS facing, K 2 rows to form a fold line.

Work 11 rows st st, starting with a K row.

Bind off/cast off loosely.

MAKING UP

Tidy loose ends back into their own colors. Join left shoulder seam and Neckband. Sew bound-off/cast-off edge of Sleeve top into armhole, the straight sides at top of Sleeve to form a neat right angle at bound-off/cast-off sts of armhole at Front and Back. Join rest of Sleeve and underarm seam. Fold all facings inside at fold line and hem in place. Press lightly with a warm iron over a damp cloth.

50 sts

Color Key

▨ Pale green

▨ Olive green

▨ Tarragon

☐ Pale yellow

■ Crocus

▨ Bluebell

▨ Lilac

▨ Light purple

▨ Magenta

☐ Pale pink

■ Mauve

▨ Milkshake

■ Robin

☐ Elderberry

❀ Make bobble
with Pale yellow
(see p. 169)

Wildflower Cardigan

Actual measurements:
bust 34", center neck to welt 19",
sleeve seam 17"

Gauge/tension:
28 sts and 35 rows to 4" on 3¼-mm
needles over patt

MATERIALS

- **50 g Damson silken tweed**
- **25 g Copper lurex, Twilley**
- **50 g Cornflower fine cotton chenille**
- **50 g Robin fine cotton chenille**
- **50 g Milkshake fine cotton chenille**
- **50 g Crocus fine cotton chenille**
- **50 g Toad silken tweed**
- **9 x 25 g Jet 4 ply cashmere, Jaeger**
- **1 pair 2¾-mm (US 2, UK 12) needles**
- **1 pair 3¼-mm (US 3, UK 10) needles**
- **2 stitch holders**
- **5 buttons**

INSTRUCTIONS

BACK

With 2¾-mm needles and Jet cast on 121 sts.
Work 2½" K2 P1 mock cable rib ending with a
WS row as foll:
Row 1: (P1, twist 2 knitwise) to last st, P1.
Row 2: K1 (P2, K1) to end of row.
Dec 1 st at beg of last row (120 sts).
Change to 3¼-mm needles and foll chart from bottom
to top until work measures 11" from cast-on edge,
ending with a P row.
Armhole shaping: keeping continuity of patt bind
off/cast off 6 sts at beg of next 2 rows.
Cont straight until armhole measures 8", ending with
a P row.
Shoulder shaping: keeping continuity of patt bind
off/cast off 10 sts at beg of next 6 rows.
Bind off/cast off rem 48 sts.

Cont without shaping until work measures the same as the Back up to the armhole shaping, ending with a P row.

Armhole and neck shaping: keeping continuity of patt bind off/cast off 6 sts at beg of row and K2 tog at end of row for start of neck shaping. (Place a marker at this point.)

Cont dec 1 st at neck edge on every foll 3rd row until 30 sts rem.

Work straight to match Back, ending with a P row.

Shoulder shaping: keeping continuity of patt bind off/cast off 10 sts at beg of next 3 alt rows.

RIGHT FRONT

Work as for Left Front, reversing all shapings, starting chart at st 38 and working K rows from left to right and P rows from right to left to make a mirror image.

SLEEVES

With 2¾-mm needles and Copper cast on 72 sts.
Work 1 row K2 P1 mock cable rib.
Change to Jet and work 3" K2 P1 mock cable rib, ending with a WS row and inc 8 sts evenly along the last row (80 sts).
Change to 3¼-mm needles and foll chart from bottom to top, and **at the same time,** inc 1 st at each end of every foll 6th row until there are 118 sts, taking extra sts into patt as they occur.
Work straight until Sleeve measures 17" from cast-on edge.
Bind off/cast off loosely in Jet.

POCKET LININGS (MAKE TWO)

With 3¼-mm needles and Jet cast on 26 sts.
Work 2½" st st. Leave sts on a stitch holder.

LEFT FRONT

With 2¾-mm needles and Jet cast on 61 sts.
Work 2½" K2 P1 mock cable rib ending with a WS row and dec 1 st on last row (60 sts).
Change to 3¼-mm needles and foll chart from bottom to top starting at st 19 on Row 1, **and at the same time,** place pocket on Row 1 as foll: patt 17 sts, place next 26 sts on a stitch holder and in their place patt across 26 sts of one pocket lining, patt rem 17 sts.

FRONT BANDS

Join shoulder seams.
With 2¾-mm needles and Jet and RS facing, pick up and K 1 st for each row from Right Front welt to Left Front welt.
Work 3 rows K2 P1 mock cable rib, beg with Row 2.
Next row: work 5 buttonholes evenly along band, starting first hole ½" from start of welt and last hole at start of neck shaping, and casting off 3 sts for each hole.
Next row: cast on 3 sts over the bound-off/cast-off sts in previous row.

Wildflower Cardigan

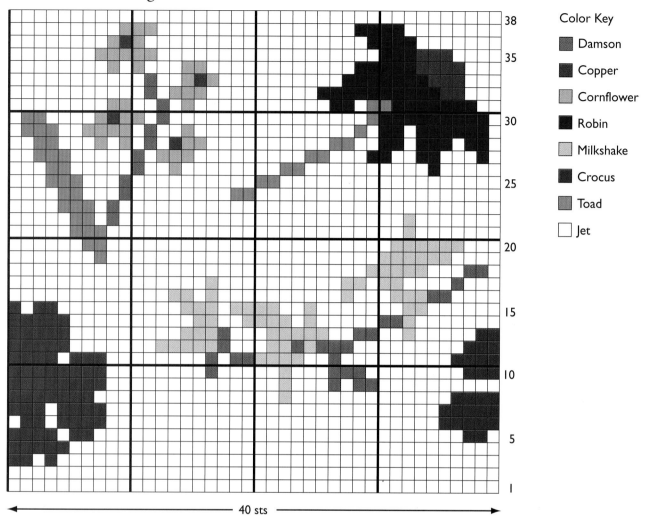

Color Key

■ Damson
■ Copper
■ Cornflower
■ Robin
■ Milkshake
■ Crocus
■ Toad
□ Jet

← 40 sts →

Work 2 rows in K2 P1 mock cable rib.
Change to Copper and work 1 row in K2 P1 mock cable rib.
Bind off/cast off in rib in Copper.

POCKET TOPS

With 2¾-mm needles and Copper work 26 sts from stitch holder in Row 2 of mock cable rib.
Bind off/cast off in P1 K1 rib in Copper.

MAKING UP

Tidy loose ends back into their own colors. Sew bound-off/cast off edge of Sleeve top into armhole, the straight sides at top of Sleeve to form a neat right angle at bound-off/cast-off sts of armhole at Front and Back. Join Sleeve and side seams. Sew Pocket Linings down. Sew on buttons to match buttonholes. Press lightly with a warm iron over a damp cloth.

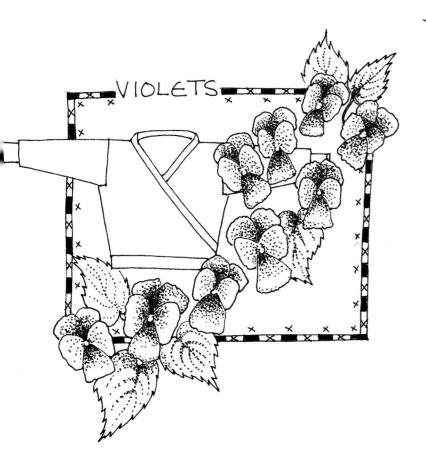

Violets Ballet Cardigan

Actual measurements:
bust 34", center back neck to welt
15½", sleeve seam 16½"

Gauge/tension:
27 sts and 34 rows to 4" on 3¼-mm
needles over body patt

MATERIALS

All yarns by Jamieson & Smith
- 25 g Lilac 4-ply Shetland
- 25 g Bluebell 4-ply Shetland
- 25 g Mauve 4-ply Shetland
- 25 g Purple 4-ply Shetland
- 25 g Turquoise 4-ply Shetland
- 25 g Bottle green 4-ply Shetland
- 25 g Misty green 4-ply Shetland
- 25 g Yellow 4-ply Shetland
- 8 x 25 g Clan green 4-ply Shetland
- 1 pair 2¾-mm (US 2, UK 12) needles
- 1 pair 3¼-mm (US 3, UK 10) needles
- 1 stitch holder

INSTRUCTIONS

BACK

With 2¾-mm needles and Clan green cast on 112 sts.
Work 1" in K1 P1 twisted rib.
Change to 3¼-mm needles and foll chart from bottom
to top and then from Row 21 to top, and **at the
same time,** inc 1 st at both ends of next and every
foll 6th row until there are 128 sts, taking extra sts
into patt as they occur.
Cont straight until work measures 7½".
Armhole shaping: keeping continuity of patt bind
off/cast off 7 sts on next 2 rows.
Cont straight until armhole measures 7½", ending
with a P row.
Shoulder shaping: keeping continuity of patt bind
off/cast off 11 sts at beg of next 6 rows.
Place rem 48 sts onto a stitch holder.

Violets Ballet Cardigan

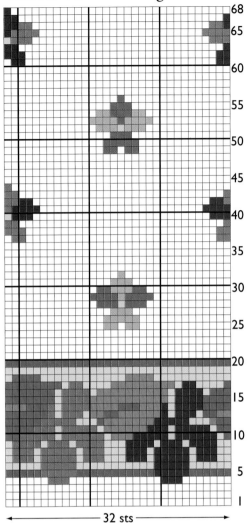

68
65
60
55
50
45
40
35
30
25
20
15
10
5
1

← 32 sts →

Color Key

☐ Lilac   ■ Bottle green

■ Bluebell   ☐ Misty green

■ Mauve   ☐ Yellow

■ Purple   ☐ Clan green

■ Turquoise

Armhole shaping: keeping continuity of patt bind off/cast off 7 sts at beg and 1 st at end of row (56 sts).

Then cont straight at armhole edge and dec 1 st at front edge on every K row until there are 47 sts.

Then dec 1 st at front edge on every alt row until there are 33 sts.

Cont straight to match Back up to shoulder shaping, ending with a P row.

Shoulder shaping: keeping continuity of patt bind off/cast off 11 sts at beg of next 3 alt rows.

RIGHT FRONT

Work as for Left Front, reversing all shapings.

SLEEVES

With 2¾-mm needles and Clan green cast on 61 sts. Work 2" K1 P1 twisted rib, increasing 3 sts evenly across last row (64 sts).

Change to 3¼-mm needles and foll chart from bottom to top once and then from Row 21, and **at the same time,** inc 1 st at both ends of next and every foll 7th row until there are 100 sts.

Cont straight until 17¼" from cast-on edge.

Bind off/cast off loosely.

BORDER

Join shoulder seams.

With 2¾-mm needles and Clan green cast on 80 sts, then pick up and K 1 st for each row from welt to shoulder on Right Front, K 48 sts on stitch holder on back neck, and K 1 st for each row from shoulder to welt; then cast on 80 sts.

Work 4 rows K1 P1 twisted rib.

Change to Purple and work 1 row K1 P1 twisted rib.

Bind off/cast off in rib in Purple.

MAKING UP

Tidy loose ends back into their own colors. Sew bound-off/cast-off edge of Sleeve top into armhole, the straight sides at top of Sleeve to form a neat right angle at bound-off/cast-off sts of armhole at Front and Back. Join rest of Sleeve and side seams. Press lightly with a warm iron over a damp cloth.

LEFT FRONT

With 2¾-mm needles and Clan green cast on 160 sts. Work 1" K1 P1 twisted rib.

Change to 3¼-mm needles and foll chart from bottom to top once and then from Row 21 to top, and **at the same time,** dec 1 st at end of every K row and 2 sts at beg of every P row until there are 85 sts and work measures same as Back to armhole.

Forget-Me-Not V-Neck Sweater

Actual measurements:

bust 44", center neck to welt 23½",
sleeve seam 18½"

Gauge/tension:

30 sts and 31 rows to 4" on 3¼-mm
needles over patt

MATERIALS

- **25 g Yellow lightweight DK**
- **2 x 25 g Aqua Shetland**
- **50 g Turquoise wool/silk**
- **25 g Lilac Shetland**
- **4 x 25 g Misty green Shetland**
- **2 x 50 g Blossom wool/silk**
- **2 x 50 g Pink DK chenille**
- **2 x 50 g Ecru fine cotton chenille**
- **4 x 50 g Ice blue wool/silk**
- **1 pair 2¾-mm (US 2, UK 12) needles**
- **1 pair 3¼-mm (US 3, UK 10) needles**
- **cable needle**
- **1 stitch holder**

INSTRUCTIONS

BACK

With 2¾-mm needles and Ice blue cast on 164 sts.
Work 17 rows cable rib as foll, rep Row 1 to Row 4:
Row 1: P2 (K4, P2) to end.
Row 2: K2 (P4, K2) to end.
Row 3: P2 (C4F, P2) to end.
Row 4: as Row 2.
Row 18: as Row 2 but inc 1 st at center of row
(165 sts).
Change to 3¼-mm needles and foll chart from bottom
to top until work measures 15" from cast-on edge.
Shape armholes: keeping continuity of patt bind
off/cast off 8 sts at beg of next 2 rows (149 sts)*.
Cont straight until armhole measures 8½", ending
with a P row.
Shape shoulders: bind off/cast off 51 sts at beg of
next 2 rows.
Bind off/cast off rem 47 sts.

FRONT

Work as for Back to *.

Neck shaping: patt 72 sts, K2 tog, turn, and leave rem 75 sts on a stitch holder.

Work 2 rows, then dec 1 st at neck edge on next row and every foll 3rd row until there are 51 sts.

Cont straight until Front measures same as Back to shoulder.

Bind off/cast off.

With RS facing, rejoin yarn to sts on holder, K2 tog, patt to end.

Complete second side to match first side, reversing all shapings.

SLEEVES

With 2¾-mm needles and Ice blue cast on 80 sts. Work 32 rows cable rib.

Change to 3¼-mm needles and foll chart from bottom to top, and **at the same time,** inc 1 st at both ends of next and every foll 5th row until there are 130 sts.

Cont straight until work measures 19" from cast-on edge.

Bind off/cast off loosely.

COLLAR

With 2¾-mm needles and Ice blue cast on 266 sts. Work 14 rows cable rib.

Shape collar: keeping continuity of rib bind off/cast off 4 sts at beg of next 44 rows.

Bind off/cast off rem 90 sts.

MAKING UP

Tidy loose ends back into their own colors. Join shoulder seams. Sew bound-off/cast-off edge of Sleeve top into armhole, the straight sides at top of Sleeve to form a neat right angle at bound-off/cast-off sts of armhole at Front and Back. Join rest of Sleeve and underarm seam. Attach Collar to neck. Press lightly with a warm iron over a damp cloth.

Forget-Me-Not V-Neck Sweater

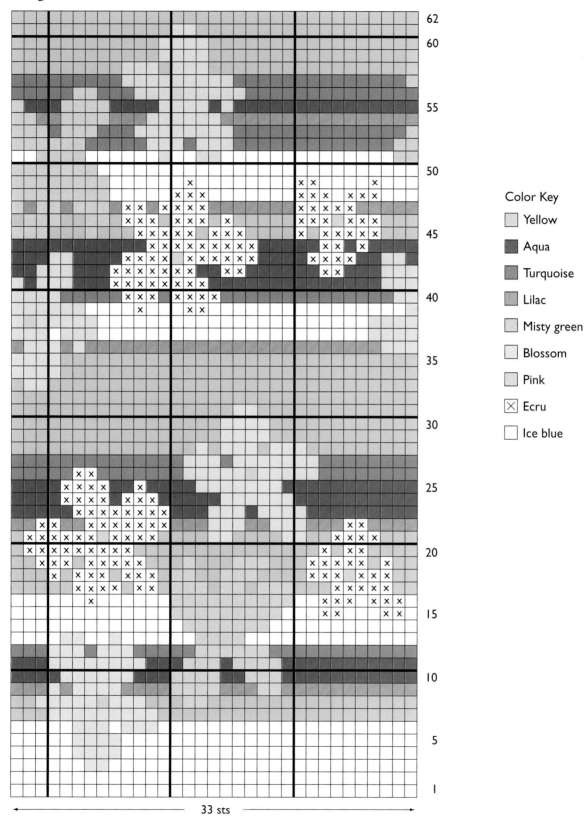

33 sts

Color Key

- ▢ Yellow
- ■ Aqua
- ■ Turquoise
- ▨ Lilac
- ▨ Misty green
- ▢ Blossom
- ▢ Pink
- ⊠ Ecru
- ▢ Ice blue

Garlands Round-Neck Cardigan

Actual measurements:
bust 41", center back neck to welt 18",
sleeve seam 13"

Gauge/tension:
27½ sts and 34½ rows to 4" on 3¼-mm
needles over patt

INSTRUCTIONS

BACK

Frill: with 2¾-mm needles and Ecru cast on 424 sts.
Row 1: P1 (K7 P2) to end.
Row 2: (K2 P7) to last st, K1.
Row 3: P1 (sl 1 K1 psso K3 K2 tog P2) to end (330 sts).
Row 4: (K2 P5) to last st, K1.
Row 5: P1 (sl 1 K1 psso K1 K2 tog P2) to end (236 sts).
Row 6: (K2 P3) to last st, K1.
Row 7: P1 (sl 1 K2 tog psso P2) to end (142 sts).
Row 8: (K2 P1) to last st, K1.
Change to 3¼-mm needles and foll chart from bottom to top until work measures 10" from cast-on edge.
Armhole shaping: keeping continuity of patt bind off/cast off 9 sts at beg of next 2 rows.
Cont straight until armhole measures 8".
Shoulder shaping: keeping continuity of patt bind off/cast off 14 sts at beg of next 4 rows and 15 sts at beg of next 2 rows.
Place rem 38 sts onto a stitch holder.

MATERIALS

- 25 g **Yellow lightweight DK**
- 2 x 50 g **Mint cotton glacé**
- 50 g **Privet fine cotton chenille**
- 50 g **Fuchsia cotton glacé**
- 50 g **Hyacinth cotton glacé**
- 10 x 50 g **Ecru cotton glacé**
- 1 pair 2¾-mm (US 2, UK 12) **needles**
- 1 pair 3¼-mm (US 3, UK 10) **needles**
- 1 **stitch holder**
- 8 **buttons**

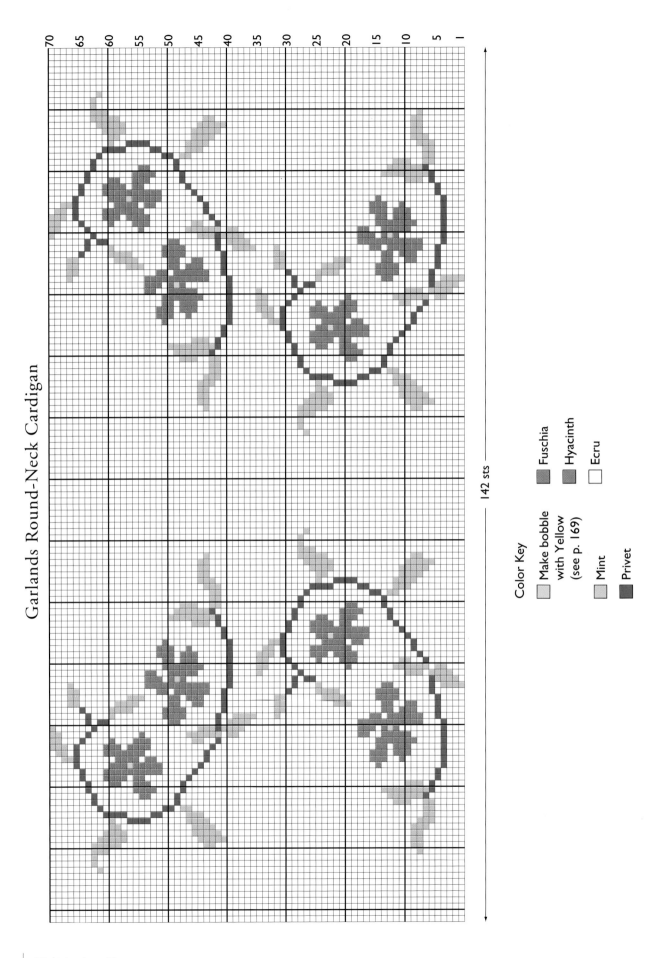

Garlands Round-Neck Cardigan

70 65 60 55 50 45 40 35 30 25 20 15 10 5 1

142 sts

Color Key

Fuschia

Hyacinth

Make bobble
with Yellow
(see p. 169)

Ecru

Mint

Privet

LEFT FRONT

Frill: with 2¾-mm needles and Ecru cast on 199 sts.
Row 1: P1 (K7 P2) to end.
Row 2: (K2 P7) to last st, K1.
Row 3: P1 (sl 1 K1 psso K3 K2 tog P2) to end (155 sts).
Row 4: (K2 P5) to last st, K1.
Row 5: P1 (sl 1 K1 psso K1 K2 tog P2) to end (111 sts).
Row 6: (K2 P3) to last st, K1.
Row 7: P1 (sl 1 K2 tog psso P2) to end (67 sts).
Row 8: (K2 P1) to last st, K1.
Change to 3¼-mm needles and foll chart from bottom to top as for Back until work measures 15" from cast-on edge, ending with a K row.
Neck shaping: keeping continuity of patt bind off/cast off 3 sts at beg of row.
Then bind off/cast off 2 sts at beg of next 2 alt rows.
Then bind off/cast off 1 st at neck edge on next 3 rows and then on next 5 alt rows (43 sts).
Cont straight to match Back to shoulder shaping, ending with a P row.
Shoulder shaping: keeping continuity of patt bind off/cast off 14 sts at beg of next 2 alt rows and 15 sts on next alt row.

RIGHT FRONT

Work as for Left Front, reversing all shapings and starting chart at st 76 in Row 1.

LEFT SLEEVE

Frill: With 2¾-mm needles and Ecru cast on 173 sts.
Row 1: P2 (K7 P2) to end.
Row 2: (K2 P7) to last 2 sts, K2.
Row 3: P2 (sl 1 K1 psso K3 K2 tog P2) to end (135 sts).
Row 4: (K2 P5) to last 2 sts, K2.
Row 5: P2 (sl 1 K1 psso K1 K2 tog P2) to end (97 sts).
Row 6: (K2 P3) to last 2 sts, K2.
Row 7: P2 (sl 1 K2 tog psso P2) to end (59 sts).
Row 8: (K2 P1) to last 2 sts, K2.
Change to 3¼-mm needles and foll chart from bottom to top, starting at st 8 on Row 1, and **at the same time,** inc 1 st at both ends of the 6th and every foll 4th row until there are 111 sts (working extra sts in Ecru only).

Cont straight until work measures 13¼" from cast-on edge, ending with a P row.
Change to 2¾-mm needles and Mint and K 1 row.
Then work 9 rows seed st/moss st.
Bind off/cast off in seed st/moss st in Mint.

RIGHT SLEEVE

Work as for Left Sleeve, except start at st 76 in Row 1.

LEFT FRONT BAND

With 2¾-mm needles and Mint pick up and K 1 st for each row from neck shaping down to bottom (not including Frill).
Work 9 rows seed st/moss st.
Bind off/cast off in seed st/moss st.

RIGHT FRONT BAND

Work as for Left Front Band, making 8 buttonholes equally spaced between top and bottom, binding off/casting off 1 st for each hole on Row 5, and in the next row casting on 1 st over the bound-off/cast-off sts in previous row.

NECKBAND

Join shoulder seams.
With 2¾-mm needles and Mint and RS facing, pick up and K 1 st for each row from halfway across Right Front Band up right side of neck, across 38 sts on holder, down left side of neck to halfway across Left Front Band.
Work 9 rows seed st/moss st.
Bind off/cast off in seed st/moss st.

MAKING UP

Tidy loose ends back into their own colors. Sew bound-off/cast-off edge of Sleeve top into armhole, the straight sides at top of Sleeve to form a neat right angle at bound-off/cast-off sts of armhole at Front and Back. Join rest of Sleeve and side seams. Sew buttons on to match buttonholes. Press lightly with a warm iron over a damp cloth, omitting frill.

Forest Fruits

Rosehip Shawl-Collar Jacket

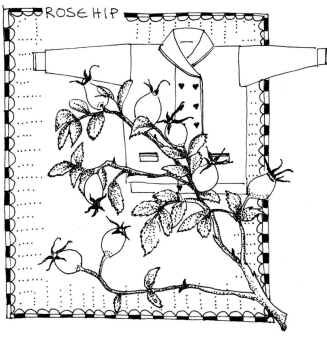

Actual measurements:
bust 48", center back neck to welt 25",
sleeve seam 20"

Gauge/tension:
22½ sts and 27½ rows to 4" on 4-mm
needles over patt

INSTRUCTIONS

BACK

With 3¼-mm needles and Swallow cast on 128 sts.
Work 2½" K1 P1 twisted rib.
Change to 4-mm needles.
Row 1: K5 in Swallow, then K 59 sts of chart from
right to left twice, K5 in Swallow.
Cont as set, foll chart from bottom to top and keep-
ing 5 sts in Swallow in st st at beg and end of each
row, until work measures 25" from cast-on edge.
Bind off/cast off.

POCKET LININGS (MAKE TWO)

With 4-mm needles and Swallow cast on 27 sts.
Work 4" in st st, ending with a P row. Leave on a
spare needle.

LEFT FRONT

With 3¼-mm needles and Swallow cast on 59 sts.
Work 2½" K1 P1 twisted rib.
Change to 4-mm needles and foll chart from bottom
for 4".

Rosehip Shawl-Collar Jacket

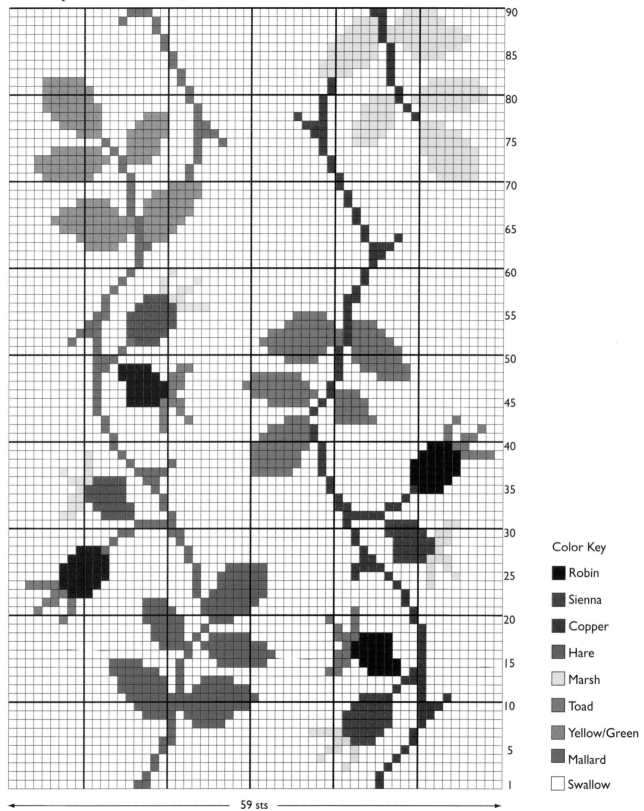

90
85
80
75
70
65
60
55
50
45
40
35
30
25
20
15
10
5
1

59 sts

Color Key

- Robin
- Sienna
- Copper
- Hare
- Marsh
- Toad
- Yellow/Green
- Mallard
- Swallow

Introduce pocket: patt 16 sts, sl next 27 sts onto a stitch holder, and in their place patt 27 sts of one pocket lining, patt rem 16 sts.

Cont without shaping until work measures 15" from cast-on edge. Place a marker at front edge to indicate start of front neck shaping (A).

Front neck shaping: Patt to last 2 sts, K2 tog.

Cont dec 1 st at neck edge on every foll alt row until 49 sts rem.

Work straight until Front matches Back, ending with a P row.

Change to Swallow and work 2" K1 P1 twisted rib. Bind off/cast off loosely in rib.

Mark halfway up the ribbing at neck edge with a contrasting thread to indicate the natural shoulder line (B).

RIGHT FRONT

Work as for Left Front, reversing all shapings, and starting with a P row (read P rows from right to left and K rows from left to right) to produce a mirror image.

SLEEVES

With 3¼-mm needles and Robin cast on 45 sts.

Work 1 row K1 P1 twisted rib then change to Swallow and work 2½" K1 P1 twisted rib.

Change to 4-mm needles and follow chart starting at st 8 on Row 1, **and at the same time,** inc 1 st at each end of the next and every foll 4th row until there are 101 sts.

Cont straight until Sleeve measures 19".

Bind off/cast off.

LEFT FRONT BAND AND COLLAR

With 3¼-mm needles and Swallow cast on 30 sts.

Work 1 row K1 P1 twisted rib*.

Place a contrasting thread at the end of this row to indicate the natural shoulder line (B).

Continue in K1 P1 twisted rib, casting on 7 sts at beg of next and foll 8 alt rows, then 11 sts at beg of foll alt row (104 sts).

Work another row in K1 P1 twisted rib so that you end up at the same side as the 11 cast-on sts.

Then take hold of Left Front and onto the same needle pick up and K 1 st for each row from marker A at start of Front shaping to cast-on edge*. Work a further 17 rows in K1 P1 twisted rib over all sts.

Change to Robin and work 1 row in twisted rib.

Bind off/cast off in rib.

RIGHT FRONT BAND AND COLLAR

With 3¼-mm needles and Swallow cast on 30 sts.

Work 2 rows K1 P1 twisted rib.

Cont as for Left Front Band from * to *.

Work a further 3 rows rib over all sts.

**Next row: Make 6 buttonholes, beg first hole after 4 sts have been worked from lower edge and last hole 4 sts from marker A, and the remainder spaced evenly between. Bind off/cast off 4 sts for each hole.

Next row: work in rib, casting on 4 sts over bound-off/cast-off sts in previous row**.

Work a further 8 rows in rib, then rep from ** to **.

Work a further 2 rows in rib.

Change to Robin, work 1 row in twisted rib.

Bind off/cast off in rib.

POCKET TOPS

With 3¼-mm needles and Swallow K 27 sts of pocket, inc 3 sts evenly across (30 sts).

Work 8 rows K1 P1 twisted rib.

Change to Robin, work 1 row twisted rib.

Bind off/cast off in rib.

MAKING UP

Tidy loose ends back into their own colors. Join shoulder seams. Sew bound-off/cast-off edge of Sleeve top into armhole, the straight sides at top of Sleeve to form a neat right angle at bound-off/cast-off edges of armhole on Front and Back. Join rest of Sleeve and side seams. Join Collar at back of neck with edge-to-edge seam on underside. Join shaped edge of Collar from center back of neck, alongside rib at shoulder, matching contrasting threads B, and down Left Front to start of front edge shaping, with edge-to-edge seam. Join right side to match. Join sides of Pocket Tops to main work. Sew down Pocket Linings. Fold back shawl collar. Sew on buttons to match buttonholes. Press lightly with a warm iron over damp cloth.

Rosehip Tam-o'-Shanter

Actual measurements:
headband 21"

Gauge/tension:
19 sts and 28 rows to 4" on 4-mm
needles over st st

MATERIALS

- **50 g Swallow DK tweed**
- **Leftover Swallow and Robin from jacket**
- **1 set of four 3¼-mm (US 3, UK 10) double-pointed needles**
- **1 set of four 4-mm (US 6, UK 8) double-pointed needles**

INSTRUCTIONS

With 4-mm double-pointed needles and Swallow cast on 8 sts

Round 1: (yo K1) to end of round.
Round 2: (yo K2 tog) to end of round.
Round 3: (yo K2) to end of round.
Round 4: (yo K1 K2 tog) to end of round.
Round 5: (yo K3) to end of round.
Round 6: (yo K2 K2 tog) to end of round.
Round 7: (yo K4) to end of round.
Round 8: (yo K3 K2 tog) to end of round.
Round 9: (yo K5) to end of round.
Round 10: (yo K4 K2 tog) to end of round.
Round 11: (yo K6) to end of round.
Round 12: (yo K5 K2 tog) to end of round.
Round 13: (yo K7) to end of round.
Round 14: (yo K6 K2 tog) to end of round.
Round 15: (yo K8) to end of round.
Round 16: (yo K7 K2 tog) to end of round.
Round 17: (yo K9) to end of round.
Round 18: (yo K8 K2 tog) to end of round.
Round 19: (yo K10) to end of round.
Round 20: (yo K9 K2 tog) to end of round.
Round 21: (yo K11) to end of round.
Round 22: (yo K10 K2 tog) to end of round.
Round 23: (yo K12) to end of round.
Round 24: (yo K11 K2 tog) to end of round.
Round 25: (yo K13) to end of round.
Round 26: (yo K12 K2 tog) to end of round.
Round 27: (yo K14) to end of round.
Round 28: (yo K13 K2 tog) to end of round.
Round 29: (yo K15) to end of round.
Round 30: (yo K14 K2 tog) to end of round.
Round 31: (yo K16) to end of round.
Round 32: (yo K15 K2 tog) to end of round.
Round 33: (yo K17) to end of round.
Round 34: (yo K16 K2 tog) to end of round.

Round 35: (yo K18) to end of round.
Round 36: (yo K17 K2 tog) to end of round.
Round 37: (yo K19) to end of round (160 sts).
Change to Robin and K to end of round.
Next round: P to end.
Change to Swallow and K st st rounds for 2½".
Change to 3¼-mm double-pointed needles and (K2 tog) to end of round (80 sts).
Work 1½" K1 P1 twisted rib.
Change to Robin and K 1 round.
Bind off/cast off loosely in Robin.
Make a pompom in Robin (see p. 168).
Tidy loose ends back into their own colors. Attach pompom to cast-on sts.

Hawthorn Berries Jacket

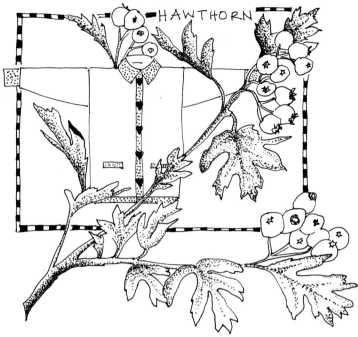

Actual measurements:
bust 52", center back neck to welt 31",
sleeve seam 17"

Gauge/tension:
20 sts and 24 rows to 4" on 4½-mm needles
over patt

INSTRUCTIONS

BACK

With 4-mm needles and Raven cast on 132 sts.
Work 2" in seed st/moss st.
Change to 4½-mm needles and foll chart from bottom
to top twice and then from Row 1 to Row 22 (166
rows).
Shoulder shaping: keeping continuity of patt bind
off/cast off 15 sts at beg of next 6 rows.
Bind off/cast off rem 42 sts.

POCKET LININGS (MAKE TWO)

With 4-mm needles and Raven cast on 24 sts. Work
6" in st st.
Place onto a spare needle.

LEFT FRONT

With 4-mm needles and Raven cast on 66 sts.
Work 2" seed st/moss st.
Change to 4½-mm needles and foll chart from bottom
up to and including Row 36.

MATERIALS

- 50 g Robin fine cotton chenille
- 50 g Hare DK tweed
- 50 g Skye DK tweed
- 2 x 100 g Forest green chunky chenille
- 100 g Lush chunky chenille
- 100 g Maple chunky chenille
- 100 g Fern chunky chenille
- 100 g French mustard chunky chenille
- 100 g Sienna magpie tweed
- 8 x 100 g Raven magpie Aran
- 1 pair 4-mm (US 6, UK 8) needles
- 1 pair 4½-mm (US 7, UK 7) needles
- 2 stitch holders
- 6 buttons

Hawthorn Berries Jacket and Throw

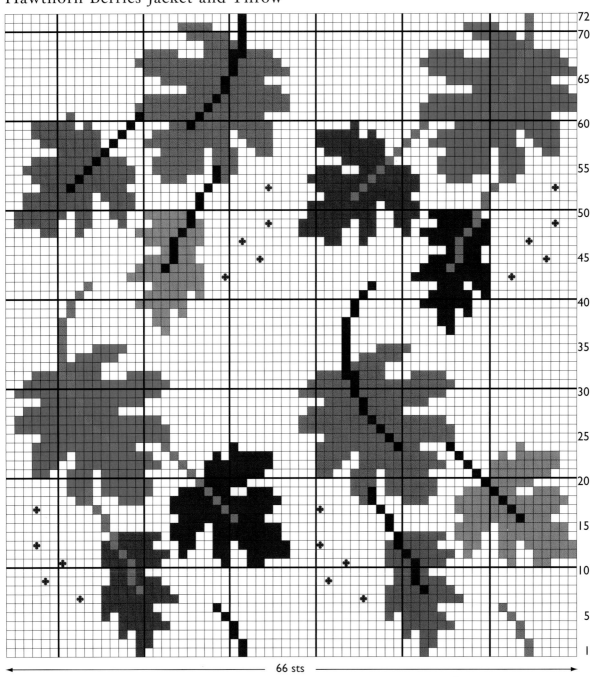

72
70
65
60
55
50
45
40
35
30
25
20
15
10
5
1

66 sts

Color Key

Hare   Fern

Skye   French mustard

Forest green   Sienna

Lush   Raven

Maple   ✤ Make bobble with Robin (see p. 169)

Row 37, introduce pocket: Patt across 21 sts, place 24 sts onto a stitch holder, then K across 24 sts of pocket lining, and then patt across rem 21 sts.
Cont up to and including Row 1 on third working of chart.
Row 2, neck shaping (WS): bind off/cast off 4 sts, patt to end.
Then dec 1 st at neck edge on next 17 rows.
Shoulder shaping: keeping continuity of patt bind off/cast off 15 sts at beg of next 3 alt K rows.

RIGHT FRONT

Work as for Left Front, reversing all shapings and starting chart at st 1 with a P row to produce a mirror image.

SLEEVES

With 4-mm needles and Forest green cast on 38 sts loosely.
Work 2¾" seed st/moss st.
Next row: P to form a fold line.
Change to Raven and work 2½" st st, starting with a P row and ending with a P row.
Next row: K, inc 28 sts evenly across row (66 sts).
(**Note:** the RS of the cuff is the reverse st st.)
Change to 4½-mm needles and foll chart from bottom starting with a K row, and **at the same time,** inc 1 st at both ends of every foll 5th row until there are 94 sts.
Cont straight to and including Row 72 and then from Row 1 to Row 13.
Bind off/cast off loosely.

LEFT FRONT BAND

With 4-mm needles and Raven and RS facing, pick up and K 7 sts for each 8 rows from neck to welt.
Work 8 rows in seed st/moss st.
Bind off/cast off in seed st/moss st.

RIGHT FRONT BAND

Work as for Left Band, but work 6 buttonholes evenly along center of band, binding off/casting off 3 sts for each hole, and on next row casting on 3 sts over the bound-off/cast-off sts of previous row.

POCKET TOPS

With 4-mm needles and Forest green K across 24 sts of pocket.
Work 1" seed st/moss st.
Bind off/cast off in seed st/moss st.

COLLAR

With 4-mm needles and Forest green cast on 36 sts.
Working in seed st/moss st throughout, work 1 row.
Cast on 11 sts at beg of next 4 rows (80 sts).
Continue on these sts for 2½".
Bind off/cast off loosely in seed st/moss st.

MAKING UP

Tidy loose ends back into their own colors. Join shoulder seams. With center of Sleeve top at shoulder seam, set in Sleeve. Join rest of Sleeve and side seams. Turn chenille cuffs to outside at fold line and sew to last row of facing. Sew on Collar, shaped edge to neck, beg and ending at inside front bands. Sew down pocket facings. Sew buttons to match buttonholes. Press lightly with a warm iron over a damp cloth.

Hawthorn Berries Throw

Actual measurements :
60" × 44"

Gauge/tension:
20 sts and 24 rows to 4" on 4½-mm
needles over patt

INSTRUCTIONS

CENTER

With 4-mm needles and Raven cast on 198 sts.
Work 1½" seed st/moss st.
Change to 4½-mm needles and foll chart from bottom
to top 5 times.
Change to 4-mm needles and work 1½" seed st/moss
st in Raven.
Bind off/cast off.

SIDE BORDERS

With 4-mm needles and Raven, starting at top left
corner, pick up and K 7 sts for each 8 rows along left
side of throw to bottom left corner.
Work 1½" seed st/moss st.
Bind off/cast off in seed st/moss st.
Work right side border in the same manner, starting
at bottom right corner and finishing at top right
corner.

LATTICE FRINGING

Using Raven cut thirty-three 10"-long tassels (with
4 lengths of yarn for each tassel).
Attach tassels to top of throw at approx 1¼" intervals.
Then foll instructions for Lattice Fringe on p. 168.
Work bottom of throw in the same manner.
Tidy loose ends back into their own colors. Press
lightly with a warm iron over a damp cloth.

MATERIALS

- **50 g Robin fine cotton chenille**
- **50 g Hare DK tweed**
- **50 g Skye DK tweed**
- **100 g Forest green chunky chenille**
- **100 g Lush chunky chenille**
- **100 g Fern chunky chenille**
- **100 g French mustard chunky chenille**
- **100 g Sienna magpie tweed**
- **100 g Maple chunky chenille**
- **10 x 100 g Raven magpie Aran**
- **I pair 4-mm (US 6, UK 8) needles**
- **I pair 4½-mm (US 7, UK 7) needles**

Rowanberry
Cropped Jacket

Actual measurements:
bust 38", center back neck to welt
19", sleeve seam 19"

Gauge/tension:
22 sts and 30½ rows over 4" on
3¾-mm needles over st st

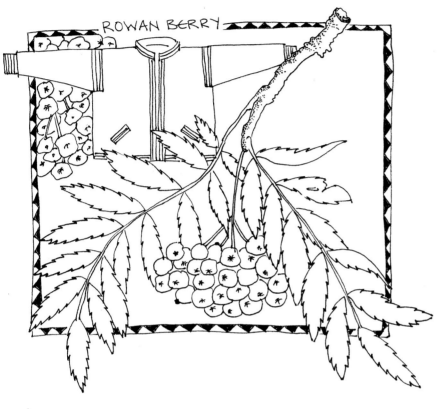

INSTRUCTIONS

BACK

With 2¾-mm needles and Peat cast on 104 sts.
Work 9 rows K1 P1 twisted rib in foll stripe
sequence:
Row 1: Damson.
Row 2: Robin.
Row 3: Peat.
Change to 3¾-mm needles and Forest and work in st
st until work measures 10" from cast-on edge.
Introduce motif: K32 Forest, patt 40 from chart, K32
Forest.
Cont as set up to and including Row 6 of chart.
Shape armholes: keeping continuity of patt bind
off/cast off 11 sts at beg of next 2 rows.
Continue to top of chart.
Continue in st st in Forest until work measures 17"
from cast-on edge, ending with a P row.
K 1 row Peat.

MATERIALS

- 50 g Robin fine cotton chenille
- 100 g Sienna magpie Aran
- 50 g Sap green DDK
- 50 g Damson silken tweed
- 50 g Peat DK tweed
- 7 x 50 g Forest silken tweed
- 1 pair 2¾-mm (US 2, UK 12) needles
- 1 pair 3¾-mm (US 5, UK 9) needles
- 1 stitch holder

Rowanberry Cropped Jacket

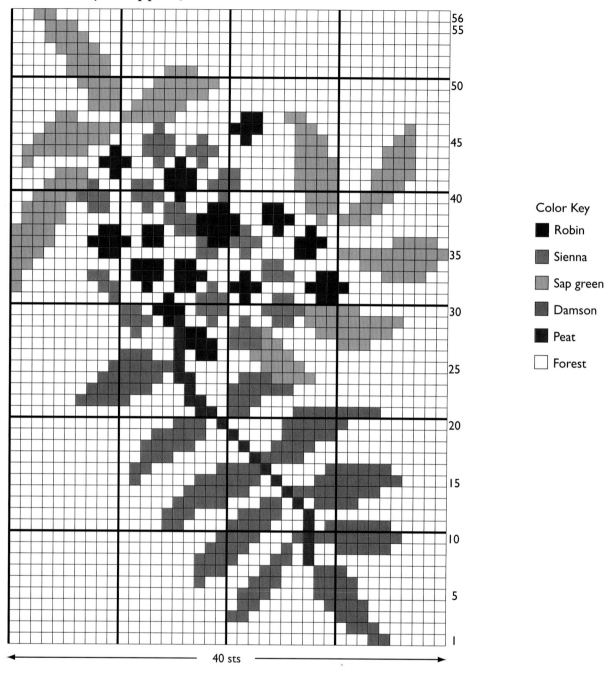

Color Key

- ■ Robin
- ■ Sienna
- ■ Sap green
- ■ Damson
- ■ Peat
- □ Forest

LEFT FRONT

Work 9 rows in K1 P1 twisted rib in stripe sequence. Keeping in stripe sequence, bind off/cast off 24 sts at beg of next 2 rows in rib.

Place rem 34 sts onto a stitch holder.

With 2¾-mm needles and Peat cast on 55 sts.
Work 9 rows K1 P1 twisted rib in stripe sequence, and **at the same time**, dec 1 st at left edge on next and every foll row (46 sts).
Change to 3¾-mm needles and Forest and work 2" st st, ending with a P row.

Introduce pocket: K15, turn, leaving rem 31 sts on a spare needle.

Working on these 15 sts for 16 rows, inc 1 st at left edge on every row, so that the pocket slit slopes from right to left.

Return to the 31 sts on spare needle, K 1 row.

Then work 16 rows, dec 1 st at right edge on every row.

Work across all 46 sts.

Cont straight until Front measures same as Back to armhole, ending with a P row.

Armhole shaping: bind off/cast off 11 sts at beg of next row.

Cont straight until work measures 14" from cast-on edge, ending with a K row.

Neck shaping: bind off/cast off 1 st at neck edge on next and foll 10 alt rows (24 sts).

Work 10 rows in K1 P1 twisted rib in stripe sequence, starting with Peat. Bind off/cast off in rib with Peat.

RIGHT FRONT

Work as for Left Front, reversing all shapings and starting pocket 31 sts from center front and making it slope from left to right by dec on right side and inc on left side.

SLEEVE

With 2¾-mm needles and Peat cast on 42 sts.

Work 15 rows K1 P1 twisted rib in stripe sequence. Change to 3¾-mm needles and Forest and st st, inc 1 st at both ends of next and every foll 4th row until there are 102 sts.

Cont straight until work measures 18¾" from cast-on edge, ending with a P row.

Work 10 rows in stripe sequence, starting with Peat. Bind off/cast off in Peat in rib.

FRONT BORDERS

With 2¾-mm needles and Peat and RS of Right Front facing, pick up and K 1 st for each row from top of welt to start of neck shaping. Work 9 rows K1 P1 twisted rib in the reverse stripe sequence (Robin, Damson, Peat), and **at the same time,** inc 1 st at welt

end of each row and join to matching bound-off/cast-off sts of welt on each row to form a mitred corner.

Bind off/cast off in rib in Peat.

Work border on Left Front to match.

NECKBAND

Join shoulder seams.

With 2¾-mm needles and Peat and RS facing, pick up and K 1 st for each row from halfway across Right Front Border, up right neck, across 34 sts on holder at back of neck, down left neck to halfway across Left Front Border. Work 9 rows K1 P1 twisted rib in reverse stripe sequence.

Bind off/cast off in rib in Peat.

POCKET TOPS

With 2¾-mm needles and Forest and RS facing, pick up and K 24 sts across edge nearest Front Border. Work 8 rows K1 P1 twisted rib in stripe sequence. Bind off/cast off in rib in Peat.

POCKET LININGS

With 3¾-mm needles and Forest and RS facing, pick up and K 22 sts across edge nearest side seam. Work 2" in st st. Bind off/cast off.

MAKING UP

Tidy loose ends back into their own colors. Sew bound-off/cast-off edge of Sleeve top into armhole, the straight sides at top of Sleeve to form a neat right angle at bound-off/cast-off edges of armhole on Front and Back. Join Sleeve and side seams. Sew down Pocket Tops and sew Pocket Linings down. Press lightly with a warm iron over a damp cloth.

Blackberry Log Cabin Quilt

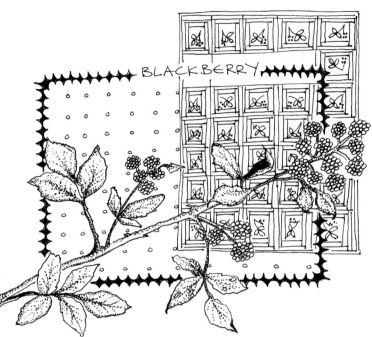

Actual measurements:
40" x 57"
Gauge/tension:
36 sts and 32 rows to 4" on 3¾-mm
needles over patt

INSTRUCTIONS

BASIC SQUARE

With 3¾-mm needles and Blood orange cast on 39 sts
Foll chart from bottom to top once.
Bind off/cast off.

LOG CABIN BORDER

Round 1: with a 0.75-mm crochet hook and Blood
orange work 1 sc/dc into each st or row around the
square, making 3 sc/dc into each corner.
Fasten off.
Work 3 rows sc/dc, putting the hook into the top two
strands of each st, in the colors indicated on the **Log
Cabin Border Diagram**; foll the number sequence
from 1 to 8.
Border 1: Pear.
Border 2: Lilac wine.
Border 3: Dijon.
Border 4: Sky blue.
Border 5: Banana.

MATERIALS

- **2 x 50 g Lilac wine cotton glacé**
- **2 x 50 g Fiesta cotton glacé**
- **3 x 50 g Kiwi cotton glacé**
- **2 x 50 g Sky blue cotton glacé**
- **2 x 50 g Dijon cotton glacé**
- **3 x 50 g Banana cotton glacé**
- **4 x 50 g Gentian cotton glacé**
- **8 x 50 g Blood orange cotton glacé**
- **2 x 50 g Pear cotton glacé**
- **1 pair 3¾-mm (US 5, UK 9) needles**
- **0.75-mm (US 12 steel, UK 13) crochet hook**

Blackberry Log Cabin Quilt

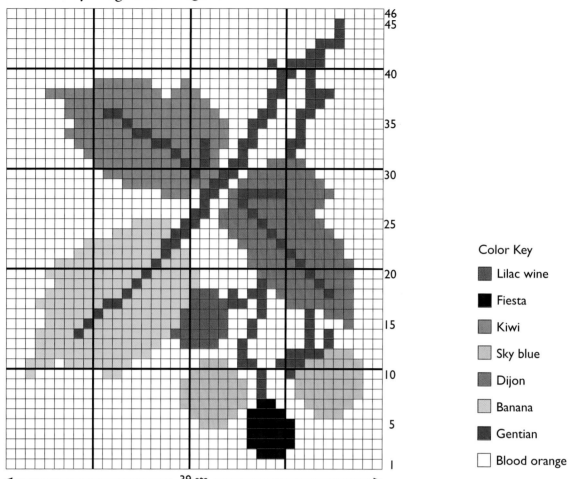

← 39 sts →

46
45
40
35
30
25
20
15
10
5
1

Color Key

■ Lilac wine
■ Fiesta
■ Kiwi
■ Sky blue
■ Dijon
■ Banana
■ Gentian
□ Blood orange

Log Cabin Border Diagram

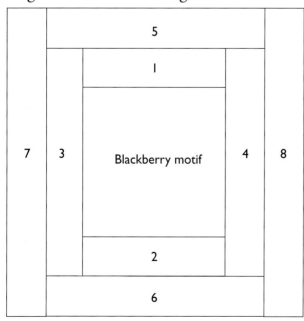

Border 6: Gentian.
Border 7: Fiesta.
Border 8: Kiwi.
Make 24 squares.

CONSTRUCTION

With a 0.75-mm crochet hook join the squares tog, 4 squares at a time (making 6 blocks of 4 squares), using Banana to join the pale sides tog and Gentian to join the dark sides tog.

Join the squares tog with sc/dc, taking the inner loop of the square facing you and the outer loop of the square behind, as shown in Joining Squares below. Foll the **Construction Diagram** for the direction in which to place each square.

Join the 6 blocks tog using same method with Banana for the pale sides and Gentian for the dark sides.

BORDER

Round 1: with a 0.75-mm crochet hook and Gentian, work in sc/dc around 4 sides of quilt putting the hook into top 2 strands of each st and making 3 sc/dc into each corner.

Round 2: 4 ch (counts as 1 hdc/htr and 2 ch) *1 hdc/htr into 3rd st along, 2 ch*. Rep from * to * around 4 sides of quilt, making 1 hdc/htr, 3 ch, 1 hdc/htr into each corner st.

Round 3 to Round 6: work as for Round 2, placing each hdc/htr on top of previous row's hdc/htr.

Tidy loose ends back into their own colors. Press lightly with a warm iron over a damp cloth.

Construction Diagram

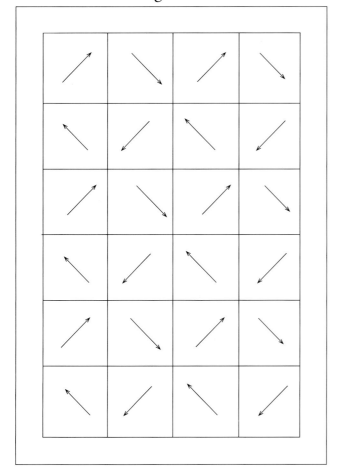

6 blocks of 4 squares

Block of 4 squares

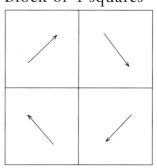

Arrows indicate direction in which blackberries should be pointed.

Joining Squares

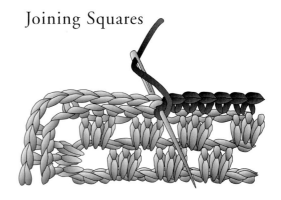

Horse Chestnut Jacket

Actual measurements:

bust 21", center back neck to welt 24",
sleeve seam 18"

Gauge/tension:

29½ sts and 32 rows to 4" on 3¼-mm
needles over patt

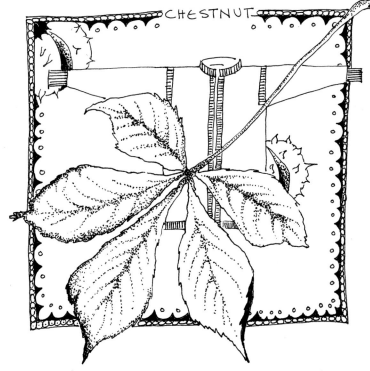

MATERIALS

- **2 x 25 g Tarragon Donegal lambswool tweed**

- **25 g Marram Donegal lambswool tweed**

- **50 g Mousse fine cotton chenille**

- **50 g Ruby fine cotton chenille**

- **50 g Marsh fine cotton chenille**

- **2 x 25 g Pickle Donegal lambswool tweed**

- **2 x 25 g Cinnamon Donegal lambswool tweed**

- **10 x 25 g Sapphire Donegal lambswool tweed**

- **1 pair 2¾-mm (US 2, UK 12) needles**

- **1 pair 3¼-mm (US 3, UK 10) needles**

- **1 stitch holder**

INSTRUCTIONS

BACK

With 2¾-mm needles and Pickle cast on 156 sts.
Work 11 rows st st, starting with a K row.
Next row: K to form fold line.
Change to 3¼-mm needles and work 10 rows bicolor rib (carrying yarn not in use on the WS of each row) as foll:
Row 1(RS): (K2 Ruby, P2 Pickle) to end.
Row 2: (K2 Pickle, P2 Ruby) to end.
Then foll chart from bottom to top up to and including Row 46 of second working of chart.
Armhole shaping: keeping continuity of patt bind off/cast off 7 sts at beg of next 2 rows.
Cont straight up to and including Row 40 of third working of chart.
Shoulder shaping: with Sapphire only bind off/cast off 17 sts at beg of next 6 rows.
Place rem 40 sts onto a stitch holder.

122

LEFT FRONT

With 2¾-mm needles and Pickle cast on 74 sts.
Work 11 rows st st, starting with a K row.
Next row: K to form fold line.
Change to 3¼-mm needles and work 10 rows bicolor rib as foll:
Row 1: (K2 Ruby, P2 Pickle) to last 2 sts, K2 Ruby.
Row 2: (P2 Ruby, K2 Pickle) to last 2 sts, P2 Ruby.
Then foll chart from bottom to top up to and including Row 46 of second working of chart.
Armhole shaping: keeping continuity of patt bind off/cast off 7 sts at beg of next row.
Cont straight up to and including Row 5 of third working of chart.
Neck shaping: keeping continuity of patt and with WS facing bind off/cast off 7 sts at beg of next row, then dec 1 st at this edge on foll 9 rows (51 sts).
Cont straight to match Back.
Shoulder shaping: with RS facing and Sapphire only bind off/cast off 17 sts at beg of next 3 alt rows.

RIGHT FRONT

Work as for Left Front, reversing all shapings.

SLEEVES

With 3¼-mm needles and Pickle cast on 60 sts.
Work 24 rows bicolor rib as foll:
Row 1(RS): (K2 Ruby, P2 Pickle) to end.
Row 2: (K2 Pickle, P2 Ruby) to end.
Then foll chart from bottom to top up to and including Row 42 of second working of chart, and **at the same time,** inc 1 st at both ends of next and every foll 3rd row until there are 120 sts, taking extra sts into patt as they occur, ending with a P row.
Change to Pickle and K 1 row.
Then with RS facing, work 9 rows bicolor rib, starting with Row 2.
Bind off/cast off with Pickle.

FRONT BANDS (BOTH THE SAME)

With 3¼-mm needles and Pickle and RS facing, pick up and K 130 sts between welt and start of neck shaping.

Work 9 rows in bicolor rib starting with Row 2: (K2 Pickle, P2 Ruby) 32 times, K2 Pickle.
With 2¾-mm needles and Pickle only and RS facing, K 2 rows to form fold line.
Then work 11 rows st st, starting with a K row.
Bind off/cast off.

NECKBAND

Join both shoulder seams.
With 3¼-mm needles and Pickle and RS facing, pick up and K 45 sts from halfway across bicolor rib at top edge of Right Front Band, up side of neck to right shoulder, K 40 sts from back of neck, then pick up and K 45 sts down left side of neck to halfway across bicolor rib of Left Front Band (130 sts).

Horse Chestnut Jacket

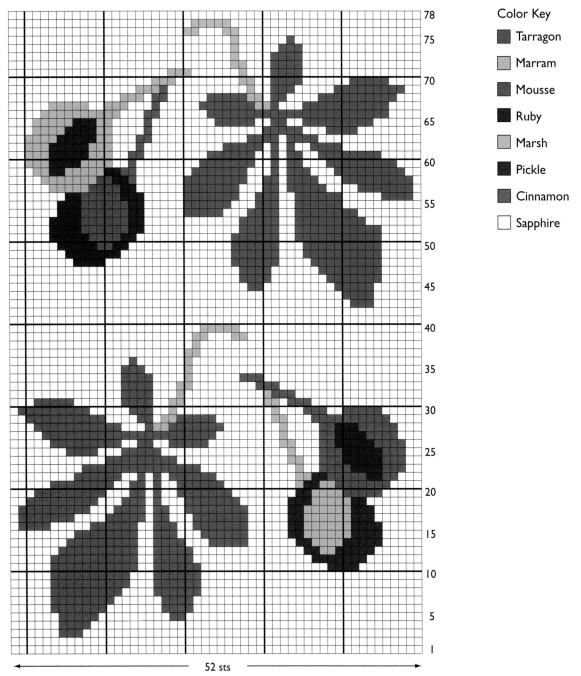

Color Key

- ◼ Tarragon
- ◼ Marram
- ◼ Mousse
- ◼ Ruby
- ◼ Marsh
- ◼ Pickle
- ◼ Cinnamon
- ☐ Sapphire

52 sts

Work 9 rows in bicolor rib, starting with Row 2: (K2 Pickle, P2 Ruby) 32 times, K 2 Pickle.
With 2¾-mm needles and Pickle only and RS facing, K 2 rows, to form fold line.
Then work 11 rows st st, starting with a K row.
Bind off/cast off.

MAKING UP

Tidy loose ends back into their own colors. Sew bound-off edge of Sleeve top into armhole, the straight sides at top of Sleeve to form a neat right angle at bound-off/cast-off edges of armhole on Front and Back. Join rest of Sleeve and side seams. Turn all facings at fold lines to inside and hem in place. Press lightly with a warm iron over a damp cloth.

Horse Chestnut Cloche Cap

Actual measurements:
headband 23½"

Gauge/tension:
24 sts and 38 rows to 4" on 3¼-mm
needles over st st

INSTRUCTIONS

Headband: With 2¾-mm double-pointed needles and Pickle cast on 140 sts.
Work 2" st st.
P 1 round to form fold line.
Change to 3¼-mm double-pointed needles and work 16 rounds bicolor rib, carrying yarn not in use on the WS of each row: (K2 Ruby, P2 Pickle) to end of round.
Crown: Change to Sapphire and work 2" st st.

MATERIALS

- **50 g Ruby fine cotton chenille**
- **25 g Pickle Donegal lambs-wool tweed**
- **25 g Sapphire Donegal lambs-wool tweed**
- **I set of four 2¾-mm (US 2, UK 12) double-pointed needles**
- **I set of four 3¼-mm (US 3, UK 10) double-pointed needles**

SHAPE CROWN

Round 1: (sl 1 K1 psso P2 K2 tog K22) 5 times.
Round 2 to Round 4: (K1 P2 K23) 5 times.
Round 5: (sl 1 K1 psso P2 K2 tog K20) 5 times.
Round 6 to Round 8: (K1 P2 K21) 5 times.
Round 9: (sl 1 K1 psso P2 K2 tog K18) 5 times.
Round 10 to Round 12: (K1 P2 K19) 5 times.
Round 13: (sl 1 K1 psso P2 K2 tog K16) 5 times.
Round 14 to Round 16: (K1 P2 K17) 5 times.
Round 17: (sl 1 K1 psso P2 K2 tog K14) 5 times.
Round 18: (K1 P2 K15) 5 times.
Round 19: (sl 1 K1 psso P2 K2 tog K12) 5 times.
Round 20: (K1 P2 K13) 5 times.
Round 21: (sl 1 K1 psso P2 K2 tog K10) 5 times.
Round 22: (K1 P2 K11) 5 times.
Round 23: (sl 1 K1 psso P2 K2 tog K8) 5 times.

Round 24: (K1 P2 K9) 5 times.
Round 25: (sl 1 K1 psso P2 K2 tog K6) 5 times.
Round 26: (sl 1 K1 psso P2 K2 tog K4) 5 times.
Round 27: (sl 1 K1 psso P2 K2 tog K2) 5 times.
Round 28: (sl 1 K1 psso P2 K2 tog) 5 times.
Round 29: (K2 tog P2) 5 times.
Round 30: (K1 P2 tog) 5 times.
Round 31: (K2 tog) 5 times.
Break yarn off and draw through rem 5 sts and fasten off.

MAKING UP

Turn headband lining to inside at fold line and sew down.

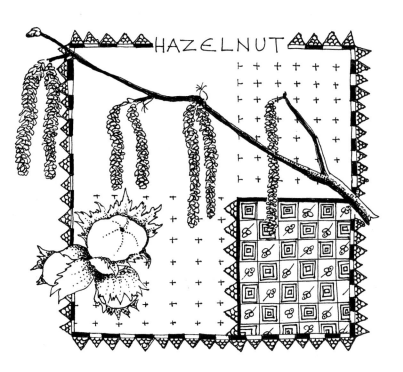

Hazelnut Throw

Actual measurements:
57" x 30"

Gauge/tension:
23½ sts and 28 rows to 4" on 3¾-mm
needles over patt

INSTRUCTIONS

Make 42 knitted squares as foll:

With 3¾-mm needles and Wren cast on 25 sts.

Foll chart from bottom to top once, being careful not to let the background yarn pull as it is being woven behind the motif.

Bind off/cast off.

Tidy loose ends back into their own colors.

Make 42 crochet squares as foll:

With 3-mm crochet hook and Peat make a 4 ch base ring and join with sl st.

Round 1: 5 ch (count as 1 dc/tr and 2 ch), (3 dc/tr into ring, 2 ch) 3 times, 1 dc/tr into ring, sl st to 3rd of 5 ch (4 groups of 3 dc/tr).

Round 2: sl st into next ch, 7 ch (count as 1 dc/tr and 4 ch)*, 2 dc/tr into same arch, 1 dc/tr into each dc/tr across side of square**, 2 dc/tr into next arch, 4 ch. Rep from * twice and from * to ** again, 1 dc/tr into same arch as 7 ch, sl st to 3rd of 7 ch (4 groups of 7 dc/tr).

Round 3: as Round 2 (4 groups of 11 dc/tr).

Round 4: as Round 2 (4 groups of 15 dc/tr).

Round 5: as Round 2 (4 groups of 19 dc/tr).

MATERIALS

- **50 g Copper silken tweed**
- **2 x 50 g Robin fine cotton chenille**
- **50 g Catkin fine cotton chenille**
- **50 g Toad silken tweed**
- **9 x 50 g Peat DK tweed**
- **5 x 50 g Wren DK tweed**
- **1 pair 3¾-mm (US 5, UK 9) needles**
- **3-mm (US D/3, UK 9) crochet hook**

127

Hazelnut Throw

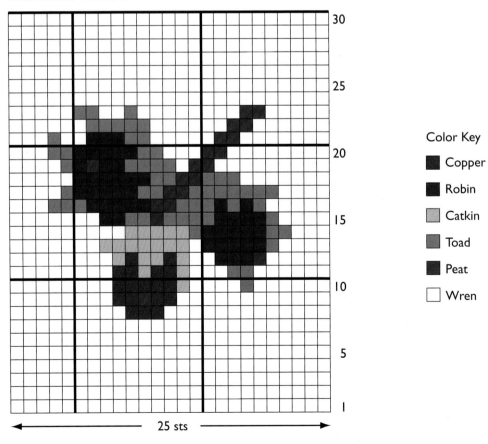

Color Key

■ Copper

■ Robin

▨ Catkin

▨ Toad

■ Peat

☐ Wren

25 sts

Crochet Square

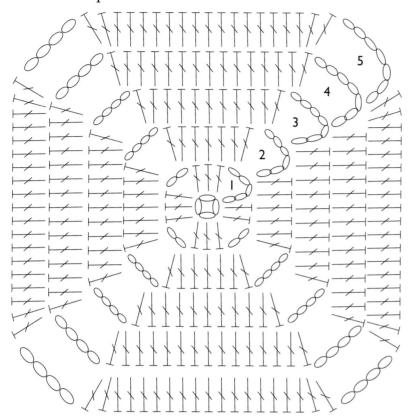

CONSTRUCTION

With 3-mm crochet hook and Robin join squares tog with sc/dc, as shown in Joining Squares on p. 121 and the Construction Diagram on p. 130.
Then work 1 row sc/dc around with Peat.
Next round: with Peat work 1 row dc/tr around 4 sides of throw making 3 ch in each corner.
Then work half diamonds at top and bottom of throw as foll:
With Copper and RS facing, work 1 row tr/dc across top (bottom) edge.
Row 1: Turn, *5 ch, sl st into top 2 loops of 4th tr/dc along, 5 ch, sl st into 4th tr/dc along*. Rep from * to * 4 more times (should be at end of Peat crochet square) for a total of 6 arches.
Row 2: Turn, sl st up side of ch arch twice, 5 ch, sl st into top of next arch, *5 ch, sl st into top of next arch*. Rep from * to * 3 more times (5 arches).
Row 3: Turn, sl st up side of ch arch twice, 5 ch, sl st into top of next arch, *5 ch, sl st into top of next arch*. Rep from * to * 2 more times (4 arches).

Row 4: Turn, sl st up side of ch arch twice, 5 ch, sl st into top of next ch arch, *5 ch, sl st into top of next arch*. Rep from * to * once (3 arches).
Row 5: Turn, sl st up side of ch arch twice, 5 ch, sl st into top of next ch arch, 5 ch sl st into top of next ch arch (2 arches).
Row 6: Turn, sl st up side of ch arch twice, 5 ch, sl st into top of next arch (1 arch). Secure with tr/dc.
Break off yarn.
Join yarn to next tr/dc along on top (bottom) edge of throw.
Work half diamond, from Row 1 to Row 6, 6 more times.
Half diamond trim: with Robin and RS facing, work 1 row tr/dc along edges of half diamonds, making 3 tr/dc into the top of each diamond point and tidying in loose ends as you go.
Press lightly with a warm iron over a damp cloth on WS of throw.

Construction Diagram

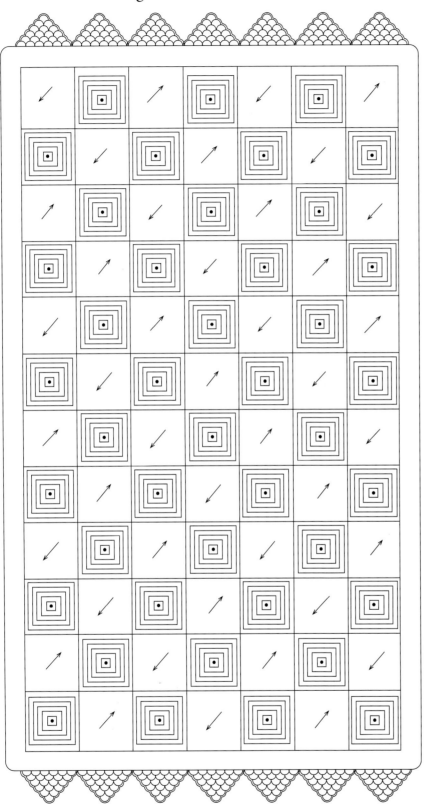

 = Crochet square

Arrows indicate direction in which hazelnuts should be pointed.

Sloe berries
Chunky Jacket

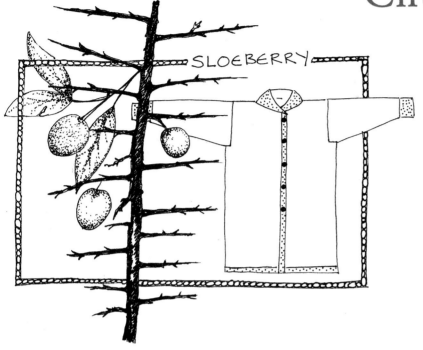

SLOEBERRY

Actual measurements:
bust 54", center back neck to
welt 29", sleeve seam

Gauge/tension:
19½ sts and 23½ rows to 4" on
4½-mm needles over patt

MATERIALS

- 100 g **Ember magpie tweed**
- 50 g **Ruby fine cotton chenille**
- 100 g **Sienna magpie tweed**
- 50 g **Crocus fine cotton chenille**
- 50 g **Plum fine cotton chenille**
- 100 g **Spark magpie tweed**
- 100 g **Forest green chunky cotton chenille**
- 100 g **Fern chunky cotton chenille**
- 100 g **Pesto magpie tweed**
- 100 g **French mustard chunky cotton chenille**
- 100 g **Aubergine chunky cotton chenille**
- 100 g **Dolphin magpie Aran**
- 9 x 100 g **Raven magpie Aran**
- 1 pair 4-mm (US 6, UK 8) needles
- 1 pair 4½-mm (US 7, UK 7) needles
- 2 stitch holders
- 6 buttons

INSTRUCTIONS

BACK

With 4-mm needles and Raven cast on 132 sts.
Work 2" in seed st/moss st.
Change to 4½-mm needles and foll chart from bottom to top twice and again from Row 1 to Row 20 (164 rows).
Shoulder shaping: keeping continuity of patt, bind off/cast off 15 sts at beg of next 6 rows.
Bind off/cast off rem 42 sts.

POCKET LININGS (MAKE TWO)

With 4-mm needles and Raven cast on 22 sts. Work 5" st st. Place onto a spare needle.

LEFT FRONT

With 4-mm needles and Raven cast on 74 sts.
Work 2" seed st/moss st.
Change to 4½-mm needles and place last 8 sts onto a stitch holder, then foll chart from bottom to top on rem 66 sts up to and including Row 34.
Row 35, introduce pocket: patt across 22 sts, place 22 sts onto a stitch holder, then K 22 sts of Pocket Lining, then patt across rem 22 sts.
Cont with chart, omitting bobbles above pocket on Row 37, up to and including Row 57 of second working of chart.
Row 58, neck shaping: Bind off/cast off 4 sts, patt to end.
Keeping the continuity of the patt dec 1 st at neck edge on next 17 alt rows (45 sts).
Shoulder shaping: keeping continuity of patt and with RS facing, bind off/cast off 15 sts at beg of next 3 alt rows.

RIGHT FRONT

Work as for Left Front, reversing all shapings, starting chart at st 1 with a P row to produce a mirror image, and placing pocket 27 sts in from side edge. Work a buttonhole on 3rd row of welt, binding off/casting off 3 sts; and on the next row, cast on 3 sts over the bound-off/cast-off sts.

SLEEVES

With 4-mm needles and Raven cast on 38 sts.
Work 5" in seed st/moss st.
Next row: K, inc 28 sts evenly across row (66 sts).
Change to 4½-mm needles and P 1 row, then foll chart from bottom to top, and **at the same time,** inc 1 st at both ends of every foll 5th row until there are 94 sts, taking extra sts into patt as they occur.
Cont straight to Row 16 of second working of chart.
Bind off/cast off loosely in Raven.

LEFT FRONT BAND AND COLLAR

With RS facing slip sts from holder on Left Front onto a 4-mm needle, join in Raven and cont band in seed st/moss st until it fits neatly when slightly stretched up Front to beg of neck shaping, ending at outside edge.
Shape Collar: cont in seed st/moss st throughout, work 3 sts, turn, work to end.
Next row: work 4 sts, turn, work to end.
Next row: work 5 sts, turn, work to end.
Cont in same manner, working 1 st extra on each row and ending after the row: work 7 sts, turn, work to end.
Work 1 row across all 8 sts.

Sloeberries Chunky Jacket and Hat

66 sts

Color Key

- ▨ Ember
- ■ Ruby (use double)
- ▨ Sienna
- ▨ Crocus (use double)
- ■ Plum (use double)

- ▨ Spark
- ▨ Forest green
- ▨ Fern
- ▨ Pesto
- ▨ French mustard

- ■ Aubergine
- ▨ Dolphin
- ▢ Raven

✥ Make bobble with single
strand of color indicated (see p. 169)

Then inc 1 st at inside edge on every 14th row until there are 13 sts.

Cont without further shaping until collar fits up Left Front to shoulder, ending at outside edge.

With RS facing work 3 sts, turn, work to end.

Cont shaping in same manner, ending after the row: work 12 sts, turn, work to end.

Work 1 row across all 13 sts.

With RS facing, work 12 sts, turn, work to end.

Next row: work 11 sts, turn, work to end.

Cont shaping in same manner, ending after the row: work 3 sts, turn, work to end.

Working across all 13 sts, cont straight until Collar fits to center back of neck when slightly stretched. Place sts onto a stitch holder.

RIGHT FRONT BAND AND COLLAR

Work as for Left Front Band and Collar, reversing all shapings and working 5 more buttonholes evenly spaced between first buttonhole on welt and start of neck shaping; top buttonhole to start 1" below start of neck shaping. Bind off/cast off 3 sts for each hole; and on the next row cast on 3 sts over the bound-off/cast-off sts.

POCKET TOPS

With 4-mm needles and Raven, K across 22 sts of pocket, inc 1 st at each end.

Work 1" seed st/moss st.

Bind off/cast off in seed st/moss st.

MAKING UP

Tidy loose ends back into their own colors. Join shoulder seams. Join sts on holders of left and right sides of Collar tog at center back neck using Kitchener st/grafting. Sew Front Bands and Collar in place. With center of Sleeve top at the shoulder seam, set in Sleeves. Sew down Pocket Linings and sides of Pocket Tops. Sew on buttons to match buttonholes. Press lightly with a warm iron over a damp cloth.

Sloeberries Hat

Actual measurements:
headband 22"

Gauge/tension:
19½ sts and 23½ rows to 4" on
4½-mm needles over patt

INSTRUCTIONS

With 4-mm needles and Crocus (used double) cast on 76 sts loosely.

Work 1¾" seed st/moss st.

Next row: P to form fold line.

Change to Raven and work 1½" st st, starting and ending with a P row.

Next row: K, inc 56 sts evenly across row (132 sts).

Next row: P.

Change to 4½-mm needles and foll chart from Row 1 up to and including Row 37.

Next row: With Raven, P, dec 4 sts evenly across row (128 sts).

MATERIALS

- **100 g Raven magpie Aran**
- **Leftovers of all other colors from jacket**
- **1 pair 4-mm needles (US 6, UK 8) needles**
- **1 pair 4½-mm (US 7, UK 7) needles**

SHAPE CROWN:

With Raven:

Row 1: (K8, sl 1 K1 psso) to end of row.
Row 2: P.
Row 3: (K7, sl 1 K1 psso) to end of row.
Row 4: P.
Row 5: (K6, sl 1 K1 psso) to end of row.
Row 6: P.
Row 7: (K5, sl 1 K1 psso) to end of row.
Row 8: P.
Row 9: (K4, sl 1 K1 psso) to end of row.
Row 10: P.
Row 11: (K3, sl 1 K1 psso) to end of row.
Row 12: P.

Row 13: (K2, sl 1 K1 psso) to end of row.
Row 14: P.
Row 15: (K1, sl 1 K1 psso) to end of row.
Row 16: P.
Row 17: (K2 tog) to end of row.

Break off yarn, thread end through rem sts. Draw up and secure.

Tidy loose ends back into their own colors. Sew side seam. Fold chenille to inside at fold line and then turn chenille and 1½" Raven st st to outside to form brim.

Cottage Garden

Pussy Willow Crew-Neck Sweater

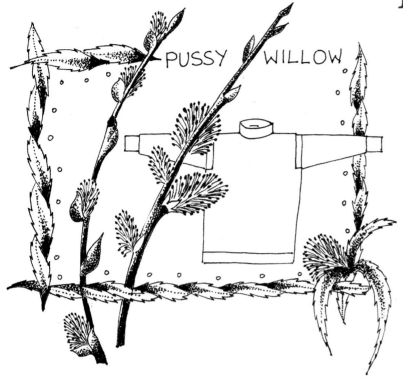

Actual measurements:
bust 50", center back neck to welt 28",
sleeve seam 16"

Gauge/tension:
26 sts and 32 rows to 4" on 3¾-mm
needles over patt

INSTRUCTIONS

BACK

With 3¾-mm needles and Black cast on 162 sts.
Work 21 rows in butterfly rib as foll:
Row 1 (WS): K1 (P6 K1) to end.
Row 2: P1 (K2 yfwd sl 2 purlwise K2 P1) to end.
Row 3: K1 (P2 sl 2 purlwise, P2 K1) to end.
Row 4: P1 (C2B, C1F, P1) to end.
Next row: work 9 sts in st st in Black, foll chart
twice, work 9 sts in st st in Black.
Work from bottom to top as set until work measures
20" from cast-on edge.
Shape armhole: keeping continuity of patt bind
off/cast off 13 sts at beg of next 2 rows.
Cont straight until armhole measures 9", ending with
a P row.
Shape shoulders: keeping continuity of patt bind
off/cast off 14 sts at beg of next 6 rows.
Leave rem 52 sts on a stitch holder.

MATERIALS

- **25 g Ochre lightweight DK**
- **2 x 25 g Gold lightweight DK**
- **50 g Pale yellow DDK**
- **25 g Olive green lightweight DK**
- **50 g Moss green DDK**
- **25 g Mistletoe green light-weight DK**
- **12 x 50 g Black DDK**
- **1 pair 3¾-mm (US 5, UK 9) needles**
- **1 pair 4-mm (US 6, UK 8) needles**
- **1 cable needle**
- **2 stitch holders**

Pussy Willow Crew-Neck Sweater

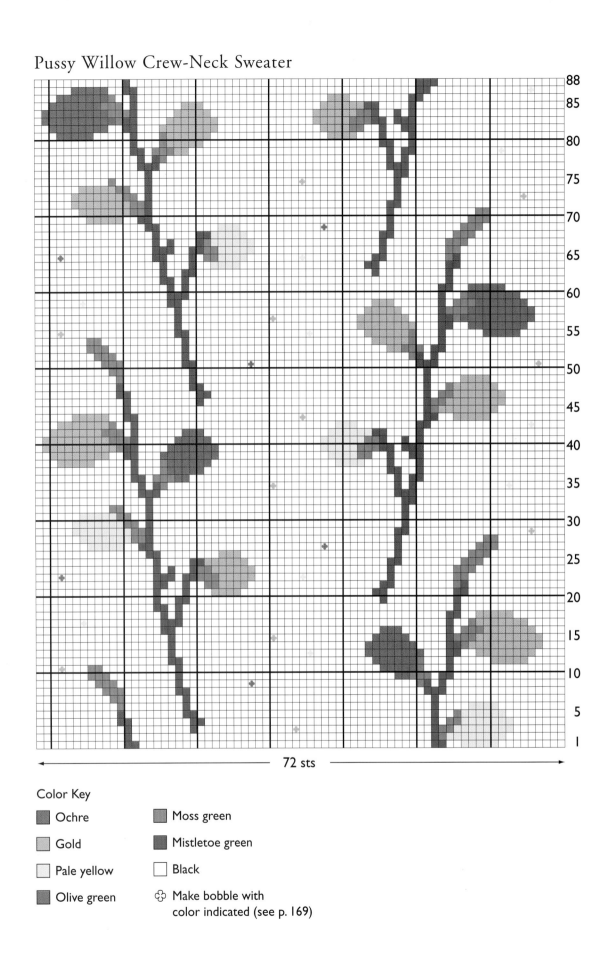

88
85
80
75
70
65
60
55
50
45
40
35
30
25
20
15
10
5
1

← 72 sts →

Color Key

■ Ochre ■ Moss green

■ Gold ■ Mistletoe green

□ Pale yellow □ Black

■ Olive green ⊕ Make bobble with
color indicated (see p. 169)

FRONT

Work as for Back until work measures 26" from cast-on edge, ending with a P row.

Shape neck: patt 62 sts, turn.

Working on these 62 sts only bind off/cast off 1 st at neck edge of every row until 42 sts rem.

Cont straight until Front measures same as Back to shoulder, ending with a P row.

Shoulder shaping: keeping continuity of patt bind off/cast off 14 sts at beg of foll 3 alt rows.

Rejoin yarn to RS of neck. Place 12 sts onto a stitch holder and then cont as for left side, reversing shapings.

SLEEVES

With 3¾-mm needles and Black, cast on 64 sts.

Work 21 rows butterfly rib.

Then foll chart from bottom to top starting at st 4 on Row 1, and **at the same time,** inc 1 st at both ends of next and every foll 4th row until there are 120 sts.

Cont straight until work measures 17", ending with a P row.

Change to 4-mm needles and Black and K 1 row.

Then work 13 rows in butterfly rib.

Bind off/cast off loosely.

NECKBAND

Join right shoulder seam.

With 3¾-mm needles and Black, pick up and K 1 st for each row down left front neck, 12 sts on stitch holder across Front, then up right front neck and across 52 sts of Back (making sure you have a multiple of 7 sts plus 1 st altogether).

Work 13 rows butterfly rib.

P 1 row to form a fold line.

Then work 10 rows st st, starting with a P row.

Cast off loosely.

MAKING UP

Tidy loose ends back into their own colors. Join left shoulder seam and Neckband. Fold Neckband facing to inside at fold line and hem in place. Sew bound-off/cast-off edge of Sleeve top into armhole, the straight sides at top of Sleeve to form a neat right angle at bound-off/cast-off sts of armhole at Front and Back. Join rest of Sleeve and side seam. Press lightly with a warm iron over a damp cloth.

Iris Round-Neck Cardigan

Actual measurements:

bust 38", center back neck to welt 21",
sleeve seam 18"

Gauge/tension:

26 sts and 32 rows to 4" on 3¾-mm
needles over patt

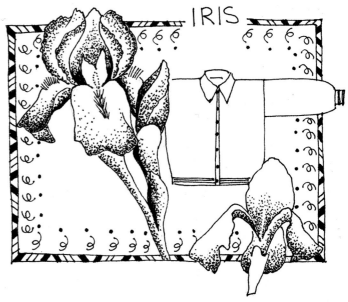

MATERIALS

- 13 x 50 g Ecru cotton glacé
- 50 g Lilac/wine cotton glacé
- 50 g Violet 4 ply cotton
- 50 g Fuchsia cotton glacé
- 50 g Candy floss cotton glacé
- 50 g Mint cotton glacé
- 50 g Tear 4 ply cotton
- 50 g Lagoon cotton glacé
- 25 g Yellow lightweight DK
- 1 pair 2¾-mm (US 2, UK 12)
  needles
- 1 pair 3¾-mm (US 5, UK 9)
  needles
- 9 buttons

INSTRUCTIONS

Note: This garment is knitted sideways.

SPECIAL INSTRUCTIONS: TRINITY STITCH

Row 1: [(P1 K1 P1) into 1st st K3 tog] to end.
Row 2: K.
Row 3: [K3 tog (P1 K1 P1) into next st] to end.
Row 4: K.
Rep Row 1 to Row 4 once and then Row 1 to Row 3 once.
Row 12: P.

BACK

With 3¾-mm needles and Ecru cast on 136 sts.
Foll chart from bottom to top for 156 rows.
Bind off/cast off.

LEFT FRONT

With 3¾-mm needles and Ecru cast on 136 sts.

Foll chart from bottom to top up to and including Row 56.

Neck shaping: keeping continuity of patt dec 2 sts at neck edge of next 16 rows (104 sts).

Change to 2¾-mm needles and Ecru and work 4 rows garter st.

Bind off/cast off.

RIGHT FRONT

With 2¾-mm needles and Ecru cast on 104 sts.

Work 4 rows garter st and, **at the same time,** work 8 buttonholes evenly along Row 2 casting off 2 sts for each hole, starting first hole 9 sts in, and on next row casting on 2 sts over bound-off/cast-off sts.

Change to 3¾-mm needles and foll chart from bottom to top starting at Row 13 and inc 2 sts at neck edge of next 16 rows (136 sts).

Cont straight until 72 rows have been completed.

Bind off/cast off.

SLEEVES

With 3¾-mm needles and Ecru cast on 110 sts.

Foll chart from bottom to top for 144 rows, starting at Row 7.

Bind off/cast off.

SLEEVE CUFFS

With 2¾-mm needles and Ecru pick up and K 64 sts for cuff, making sure the patt is running the right way.

Work 14 rows garter st.

Bind off/cast off.

COLLAR

With 2¾-mm needles and Ecru cast on 105 sts.

K 2 rows.

Next row: K2 yfwd, K to last 2 sts yfwd, K2.

K 3 rows.

Rep these last 4 rows until there are 119 sts*.

Next row: K25, turn K to end.

Next row: K18, turn K to last 2 sts, yfwd, K2.

Next row: K11, turn K to end.

Next row: K8, turn K to last 2 sts, yfwd, K2.

Next row: K6, turn K to end.

Next row: K5, turn, K to last 2 sts, yfwd, K2.

Next row: K5, turn K to last 2 sts, yfwd, K2.

Next row: K3, turn K to end.

Next row: K2, turn, yfwd, K to end.

Next row: K across all sts*.

K 1 row across all sts.

Rep from * to *.

Bind off/cast off.

MAKING UP

Tidy loose ends back into their own colors. Join shoulder seams, making sure the patt is running the right way on the Back. Position Sleeve with center of top at shoulder seam and sew in place. Join Sleeve and side seams. Attach Collar to neck.

Welts: with 2¾-mm needles and Ecru and RS facing, pick and K 275 sts along bottom edge of Back and Fronts (135 sts across Back and 70 sts across each Front).

Work 4 rows garter st, working one buttonhole to match those on Right Front on Row 2.

Bind off/cast off.

Sew on buttons to match buttonholes. Press lightly with a warm iron over a damp cloth.

Iris Round-Neck Cardigan

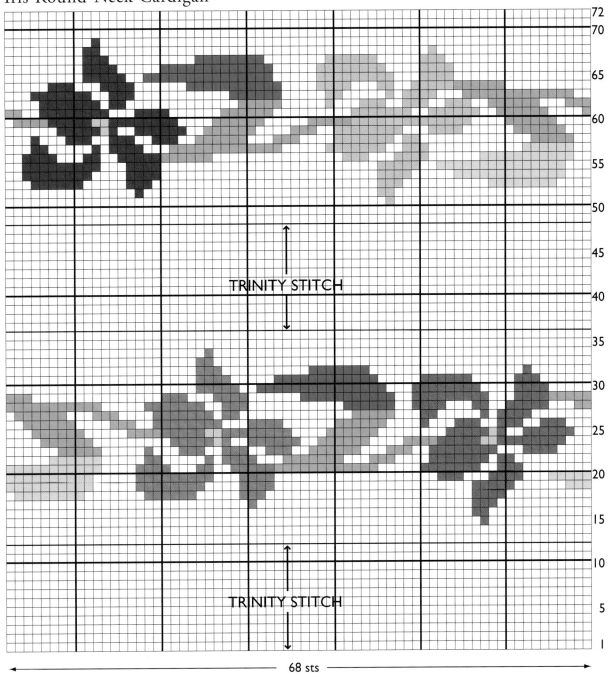

TRINITY STITCH

TRINITY STITCH

← 68 sts →

Color Key

☐ Ecru	▨ Mint
■ Lilac/Wine	☐ Tear (use double)
▨ Violet (use double)	■ Lagoon
■ Fuchsia	☐ Yellow
☐ Candy floss	

Sweet William V-Neck Jacket

Actual measurements:
bust 51", center back neck to welt 33", sleeve seam 21"

Gauge/tension:
22 sts and 29 rows to 4" on 3¾-mm needles over patt

INSTRUCTIONS

BACK

With 3¼-mm needles and Hare cast on 140 sts.
Work 16 rows in cable rib as foll:
Row 1: (P2, K4, P2, K4, P2) to end.
Row 2: (K2, P4, K2, P4, K2) to end.
Row 3: (P2, C4F, P2, C4B, P2) to end.
Row 4: as Row 2.
Change to 3¾-mm needles and foll chart from bottom to top twice, then up to and including Row 44 on the third working of chart.
Shoulder shaping: using Hare only bind off/cast off 17 sts on next 6 rows.
Bind off/cast off rem sts.

LEFT FRONT

With 3¼-mm needles and Hare cast on 84 sts.
Work 16 rows cable rib.
Change to 3¾-mm needles and work Row 1 of chart, placing last 14 sts onto a stitch holder for button band. Work rem sts up to and including Row 44.

Sweet William V-Neck Jacket

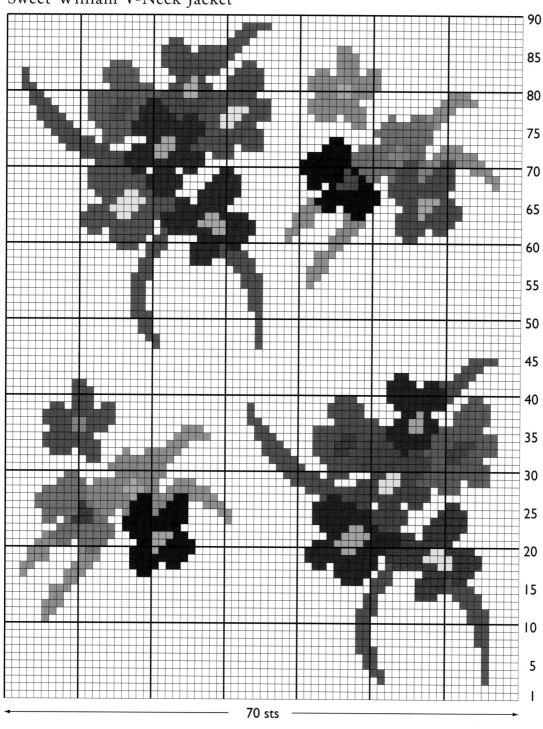

90
85
80
75
70
65
60
55
50
45
40
35
30
25
20
15
10
5
1

← 70 sts →

Color Key

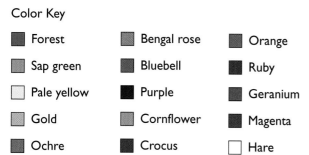

■ Forest	■ Bengal rose	■ Orange
■ Sap green	■ Bluebell	■ Ruby
☐ Pale yellow	■ Purple	■ Geranium
■ Gold	■ Cornflower	■ Magenta
■ Ochre	■ Crocus	☐ Hare

Row 45, introduce pocket: patt 21 sts, then working on next 28 sts only and Hare, work 8" st st.
Return to main work and complete Row 45.
Cont until 116 rows have been worked.
Row 117, neck shaping: keeping continuity of patt dec 1 st at neck edge on next and every foll 5th row until 51 sts rem.
Cont straight to match Back.
Shoulder shaping: using Hare only bind off/cast off 17 sts on next 3 alt rows.

RIGHT FRONT

With 3¼-mm needles and Hare cast on 84 sts.
Work 3 rows cable rib then make a buttonhole as foll:
Row 4: work to last 7 sts, turn.
Work 2 more rows cable rib on these 77 sts.
Break off yarn, join to the 7 sts and work 3 rows cable rib.
Row 7: work across all 84 sts.
Work Row 8 to Row 16 in cable rib then K 1 row.
Cont as Left Front, reversing all shapings and starting with a P row on Row 1 to produce a mirror image.

SLEEVES

With 3¼-mm needles and Hare cast on 70 sts.
Work 24 rows in cable rib.
Change to 3¾-mm needles and foll chart from bottom to top, and **at the same time,** inc 1 st at both ends of next and every foll 3rd row until there are 152 sts, taking inc sts into patt as they occur.
Bind off/cast off.

FRONT BANDS

Join shoulder seams.
Place 14 sts of Right Front Band onto 3¼-mm needles.
Work band in cable rib with Hare to fit up Front to center of back of neck.
Bind off/cast off in rib.
Return to Left Front Band and work 7 buttonholes evenly spaced between first hole and neck shaping in the same way that first hole was worked.
Cont to fit to center back neck.
Bind off/cast off in rib.

MAKING UP

Tidy loose ends back into their own colors. Position Sleeves with center top at shoulder seam and sew in place. Join side and Sleeve seams. Sew pocket sides together. Attach Front Bands and join at center back neck. Sew buttons on to match buttonholes. Press lightly with a warm iron over a damp cloth.

Poppy Cushion Cover

Actual measurements:
22" x 22"

Gauge/tension:
24 sts and 25 rows to 4" on 3¾-mm needles over patt

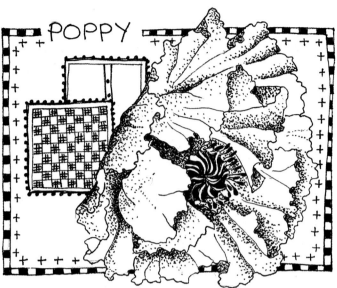

MATERIALS

- **50 g Parched fine cotton chenille**
- **100 g Black chunky cotton chenille**
- **50 g Plum fine cotton chenille**
- **50 g Robin fine cotton chenille**
- **100 g Claret chunky cotton chenille**
- **25 g Hot pink lightweight DK**
- **25 g Crimson lightweight DK**
- **100 g Raspberry chunky cotton chenille**
- **25 g Geranium lightweight DK**
- **100 g Lush chunky cotton chenille**
- **6 x 50 g Frost silken tweed**
- **1 pair 3¼-mm (US 3, UK 10) needles**
- **1 pair 3¾-mm (US 5, UK 9) needles**
- **3.50-mm (US E/4, UK 8) crochet hook**
- **18" x 18" cushion pad**
- **3 buttons**

INSTRUCTIONS

SPECIAL INSTRUCTIONS: OPEN-WORK RIB

Row 1: (K3, P1) 4 times.
Row 2: (K1, P3) 4 times.
Row 3: (m1 sl 1, K2 tog psso, m1 P1) 4 times.
Row 4: (K1, P3) 4 times.

FRONT

With 3¼-mm needles and Frost cast on 96 sts.
Work 4 rows seed st/moss st.
Change to 3¾-mm needles and foll chart from bottom to top once and then again from Row 1 up to and including Row 48.
Change to 3¼-mm needles and work 4 rows seed st/moss st.
Bind off/cast off.
Tidy loose ends back into their own colors.

BACK

Piece One
With 3¼-mm needles and Frost cast on 96 sts.

152

Work 1" seed st/moss st.

Then work 8" st st.

Now work 1½" seed st/moss st.

Bind off/cast off.

Piece Two

Work as for Piece One, making 3 buttonholes equally spaced across the 1½" seed st/moss st band, binding off/casting off 3 sts for each hole, and in the next row casting on 3 sts over the bound-off/cast-off sts.

CONSTRUCTION

With WS tog pin the Front and two Back pieces tog. Overlap Back Piece Two (with buttonholes) over Back Piece One.

With 3.50-mm crochet hook and Frost join the Front and Back pieces tog with sc/dc making 3 sc/dc into each corner and putting the crochet hook through 3 layers of fabric where the buttonhole band overlaps the button band.

Poppy Cushion Cover

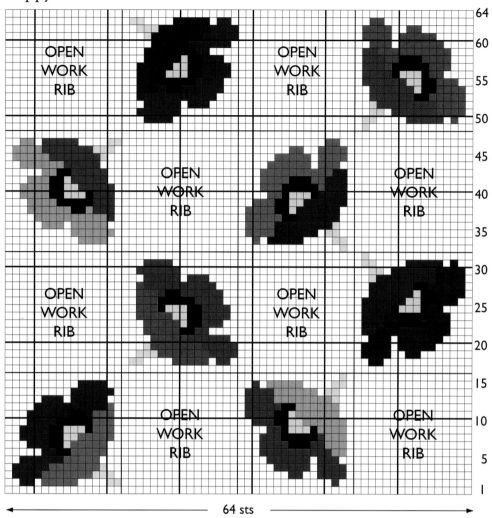

OPEN WORK RIB

OPEN WORK RIB

OPEN WORK RIB

OPEN WORK RIB

OPEN WORK RIB

OPEN WORK RIB

OPEN WORK RIB

OPEN WORK RIB

OPEN WORK RIB

64 sts

Color Key

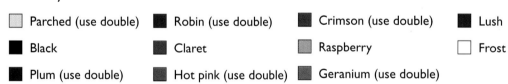

■ Parched (use double)   ■ Robin (use double)   ■ Crimson (use double)   ■ Lush

■ Black   ■ Claret   ■ Raspberry   □ Frost

■ Plum (use double)   ■ Hot pink (use double)   ■ Geranium (use double)

CROCHET CHAIN ARCH BORDER

Round 1: with a 3.50-mm crochet hook and Frost join yarn to one corner, *5 ch, sl st into 3rd sc/dc of previous row*. Rep from * to * around 4 sides of work.

Round 2: sl st up first 3 ch of previous row *5 ch, sl st into top (3rd ch along) of next arch*. Rep from * to * around 4 sides of work.

Round 3: work as for Round 2.
Fasten off.

Round 4: picot trim: join in Plum, *work 3 sc/dc along top edge of 1st arch in Round 3, 3 ch, 1 sc/dc (into same st), 3 sc/dc*. Rep from * to * around 4 sides of work.
Fasten off.
Press lightly on WS with a warm iron over a damp cloth.
Sew on buttons to match buttonholes and insert cushion pad.

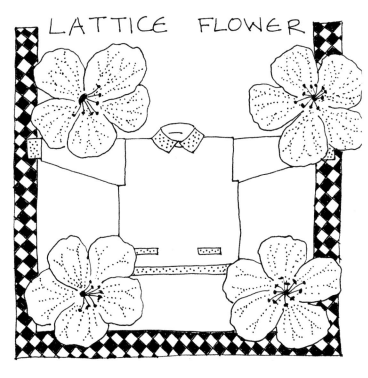

Lattice Flower Sweater

Actual measurements:
bust 46", center back neck to welt 26",
sleeve seam 16"

Gauge/tension:
25 sts and 30 rows to 4" on 3¾-mm
needles over patt

MATERIALS

- 50 g Magenta 4 ply cotton
- 50 g Petunia cotton glacé
- 50 g Lilac/wine cotton glacé
- 50 g Violet 4 ply cotton
- 50 g Ecru fine cotton chenille
- 50 g Fuchsia cotton glacé
- 50 g Catkin fine cotton chenille
- 12 x 50 g Candy floss cotton glacé
- 1 pair 2¾-mm (US 2, UK 12) needles
- 1 pair 3¾-mm (US 5, UK 9) needles
- 1 set of four 2¾-mm (US 2, UK 12) double-pointed needles
- 4 stitch holders

INSTRUCTIONS

BACK

With 2¾-mm needles and Candy floss cast on 144 sts.
Work 1" in seed st/moss st then work 1 row in st st.
Change to 3¾-mm needles and foll chart from bottom
to top until work measures 17½" from cast-on edge.
Armhole shaping: keeping continuity of patt bind
off/cast off 10 sts at beg of next 2 rows.
Cont straight until armhole measures 9".
Shoulder shaping: keeping continuity of patt bind
off/cast off 14 sts at beg of next 6 rows.
Place rem 40 sts onto a stitch holder.

POCKET LININGS (MAKE TWO)

With 3¾-mm needles and Candy floss cast on 24 sts.
Work 1¾" in st st. Leave on a spare needle.

Lattice Flower Sweater

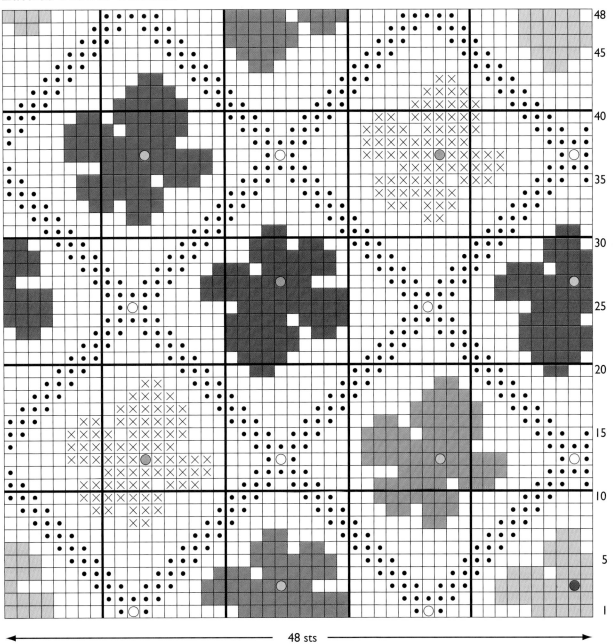

48 sts

Color Key

■ Magenta (use double)

■ Petunia

■ Lilac/Wine

■ Violet (use double)

☒ Ecru

■ Fuchsia

■ Catkin

☐ Candy floss

◯ Make bobble (see p. 169)

• P on a K row;
K on a P row
with background color

FRONT

Work as for Back up to Row 14.

Row 15, introduce pockets: patt 24 sts, place next 24 sts onto a stitch holder and in their place patt 24 sts of Pocket Lining, patt across next 48 sts, place next 24 sts onto a stitch holder, patt 24 sts of second Pocket Lining, patt rem 24 sts.

Cont as for Back, working 34 rows less than for Back.

Neck shaping: patt 58 sts, turn.

Working on these 58 sts only dec 1 st at neck edge of next 16 alt rows (42 sts).

Cont straight to match Back to shoulder shaping, ending with a P row.

Shoulder shaping: keeping continuity of patt bind off/cast off 14 sts at beg of next 3 alt rows.

Rejoin yarn to rem sts.

Place first 8 sts onto a stitch holder; then on rem sts work right front to match left, reversing shapings.

SLEEVES

With 2¾-mm needles and Candy floss cast on 48 sts. Work 1" seed st/moss st.

Change to 3¾-mm needles and foll chart from bottom to top, and **at the same time**, inc 1 st at both ends of next and every foll 4th row until there are 100 sts, taking extra sts into patt as they occur.

Cont straight until work measures 16" from cast-on edge.

Change to 2¾-mm needles and Candy floss and work 8 rows seed st/moss st.

Bind off/cast off in seed st/moss st.

COLLAR

Join shoulder seams.

With 2¾-mm double-pointed needles and Candy floss and RS facing, pick up and K 1 st for each row down left side of neck, K 8 sts on stitch holder, pick up and K 1 st for each row up right side of neck, and K 40 sts on stitch holder at back of neck.

Work 4 rounds K1 P1 rib.

Then turn at center front and work a further 2½" seed st/moss st in rows to form collar.

Bind off/cast off in seed st/moss st.

POCKET TOPS

With 2¾-mm needles and Candy floss K across 24 sts of pocket, then work 1" seed st/moss st.

Bind off/cast off in seed st/moss st.

MAKING UP

Tidy loose ends back into their own colors. Sew bound-off/cast-off edge of Sleeve top into armhole, the straight sides at top of Sleeve to form a neat right angle at bound-off/cast-off sts of armhole at Front and Back. Join rest of Sleeve and side seams. Sew down Pocket Linings and catch Pocket Tops down at sides. Press lightly with a warm iron over a damp cloth.

Anemone Wide-Neck Crew

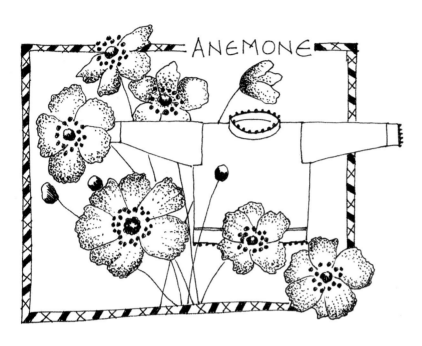

Actual measurements:
bust 45", center back neck to welt 27", sleeve seam 15"

Gauge/tension:
28 sts and 31 rows to 4" on 3¼-mm needles over patt

INSTRUCTIONS

BACK

With 2¾-mm needles and Cream cast on 155 sts.
Work 2 rows st st.
Next row: make picot edge: K1 (yfwd K2 tog) 77 times.
Work 3 rows st st.
Change to 3¼-mm needles and follow chart from bottom to top once and then from Row 20 to top until work measures 12" from picot edge line.
Armhole shaping: keeping continuity of patt bind off/cast off 12 sts at beg of next 2 rows (131 sts).
Cont straight until armhole measures 9", ending with a P row.
Shoulder shaping: keeping continuity of patt bind off/cast off 11 sts at beg of next 6 rows.
Place rem 65 sts onto a stitch holder.

Anemone Wide-Neck Crew

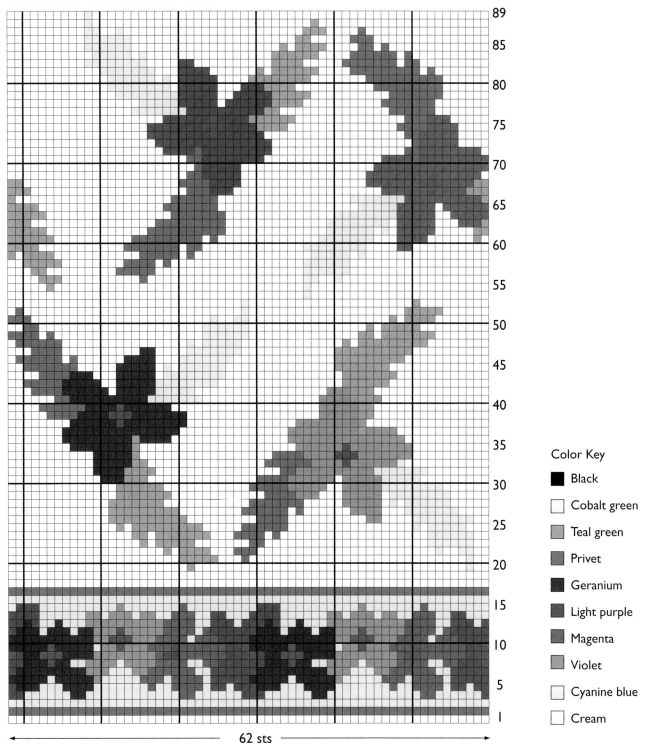

89
85
80
75
70
65
60
55
50
45
40
35
30
25
20
15
10
5
1

◄——— 62 sts ———►

Color Key

■ Black
□ Cobalt green
▨ Teal green
▨ Privet
■ Geranium
▨ Light purple
▨ Magenta
▨ Violet
□ Cyanine blue
□ Cream

FRONT

Work as for Back until work measures 15½" from picot edge line.

Neck shaping: Patt across 55 sts, turn.

Working on these 55 sts only, dec 1 st at neck edge on next and every foll 22 alt rows.

Work straight until armhole matches Back, ending with a P row.

Shoulder shaping: keeping continuity of patt bind off/cast off 11 sts at beg of next 3 alt rows.

Return to rem sts and rejoin yarn.

Place first 23 sts onto a stitch holder, patt to end.

Cont to match left side, reversing shapings.

SLEEVES

With 2¾-mm needles and Cream cast on 67 sts.

Work 2 rows st st.

Next row: make picot edge: K1 (yfwd K2 tog) 33 times.

Work 3 more rows st st.

Change to 3¼-mm needles and foll chart from bottom to top once and then from Row 20, and **at the same time,** inc 1 st at both ends of Row 17 and every foll 4th row until there are 125 sts, taking extra sts into patt as they occur.

Cont straight until work measures 18" from picot edge line.

Bind off/cast off.

NECKBAND

Join right shoulder seam.

With 2¾-mm needles and Cream and RS facing, starting at left shoulder pick up and K 1 st for each row down left side neck, 23 sts on stitch holder, 1 st for each row up right side neck, and 65 sts on stitch holder.

With WS facing work Row 2 up to and including Row 18.

Next row: make picot edge: K1 (yfwd K2 tog) to end.

With Cream only work 2¼" st st.

Bind off/cast off.

MAKING UP

Tidy loose ends back into their own colors. Join right shoulder seam. Fold Neckband at picot edge to inside and hem in place. Sew bound-off/cast-off edge of Sleeve top into armhole, the straight sides at top of Sleeve to form a neat right angle at bound-off/cast-off sts of armhole at Front and Back. Join rest of Sleeve and side seams. Fold cuff and welts at picot edge and hem. Press lightly with a warm iron over a damp cloth.

Patchwork Flowers Bedcover

Actual measurements:
55" x 82"

Gauge/tension:
22 sts and 25½ rows to 4" on 3¾-mm
needles over patt

MATERIALS

- 25 g Ultramarine lightweight **DK**
- 25 g Musk lightweight **DK**
- 16 x 25 g Venetian red **DDK**
- 50 g Robin fine cotton chenille
- 25 g Cadmium orange lightweight **DK**
- 25 g Bluebell lightweight **DK**
- 3 x 25 g Violet lightweight **DK**
- 50 g Plum fine cotton chenille
- 50 g Privet fine cotton chenille
- 2 x 25 g Turquoise lightweight **DK**
- 25 g Gold lightweight **DK**
- 25 g Tan lightweight **DK**
- 25 g Coral lightweight **DK**
- 18 × 25 g Black **DDK**
- 25 g Purple lightweight **DK**
- 1 pair 3¾-mm (US 5, UK 9) needles
- 3.50-mm (US E/4, UK 8) crochet hook

INSTRUCTIONS

BASIC SQUARE

With 3¾-mm needles and main color cast on 30 sts.
Foll chart from bottom to top once (35 rows).
Bind off/cast off.
Make 96 squares as foll:
12 Forget-me-not on Black
12 Forget-me-not on Venetian red
12 Cornflower on Black
12 Cornflower on Venetian red
12 Pansy on Black
12 Pansy on Venetian red
12 Rose on Black
12 Rose on Venetian red

CROCHET BORDER FOR SQUARES

With 3.50-mm crochet hook work in sc/dc around
each square, making 2 sc/dc into each corner.
Use Venetian red to trim the Black squares and Black
to trim the Venetian red squares.

CONSTRUCTION

With a 3.50-mm crochet hook and Black and with RS facing outward, join squares tog in vertical strips using sc/dc.
Foll **Construction Diagram** for correct placement.
Make 8 vertical strips.
Join the 8 strips tog with Black, working in sc/dc.

CROCHET BORDER FOR BEDCOVER

Row 1 to Row 3: work 3 rows sc/dc around 4 sides of bedcover with Venetian red, making 2 sc/dc into each corner.
Row 4: work 1 row dc/tr with Black around 4 sides of bedcover, making 2 dc/tr into each corner.
Row 5: work 1 row sc/dc with Violet around 4 sides of bedcover, making 2 sc/dc into each corner.
Row 6: work 1 row picot edge with Black around 4 sides of bedcover as foll: * sl st along 3 sc/dc of previous row, 3 ch, sl st into same place *. Rep from * to * to end.

Construction Diagram

F (B)	P (V)	C (B)	R (V)	P (B)	F (V)	R (B)	C (V)
P (V)	C (B)	R (V)	P (B)	F (V)	R (B)	C (V)	F (B)
C (B)	R (V)	P (B)	F (V)	R (B)	C (V)	F (B)	P (V)
R (V)	P (B)	F (V)	R (B)	C (V)	F (B)	P (V)	C (B)
P (B)	F (V)	R (B)	C (V)	F (B)	P (V)	C (B)	R (V)
F (V)	R (B)	C (V)	F (B)	P (V)	C (B)	R (V)	P (B)
R (B)	C (V)	F (B)	P (V)	C (B)	R (V)	P (B)	F (V)
C (V)	F (B)	P (V)	C (B)	R (V)	P (B)	F (V)	R (B)
F (B)	P (V)	C (B)	R (V)	P (B)	F (V)	R (B)	C (V)
P (V)	C (B)	R (V)	P (B)	F (V)	R (B)	C (V)	F (B)
C (B)	R (V)	P (B)	F (V)	R (B)	C (V)	F (B)	P (V)
R (V)	P (B)	F (V)	R (B)	C (V)	F (B)	P (V)	C (B)

Key
F = Forget-me-not
C = Cornflower
P = Pansy
R = Rose
(B) = Black background
(V) = Venetian red background

Color Key for Patchwork Flowers on p. 166
- Ultramarine
- Musk
- Venetian red
- Robin
- Cadmium orange
- Bluebell
- Violet
- Plum
- Privet
- Turquoise
- Gold
- Tan
- Coral
- Black

Color Key for Patchwork Flowers on p. 167
- Cadmium orange
- Bluebell
- Black
- Violet
- Purple
- Plum
- Privet
- Turquoise
- Gold
- Tan
- Coral
- Venetian red

Forget-Me-Not

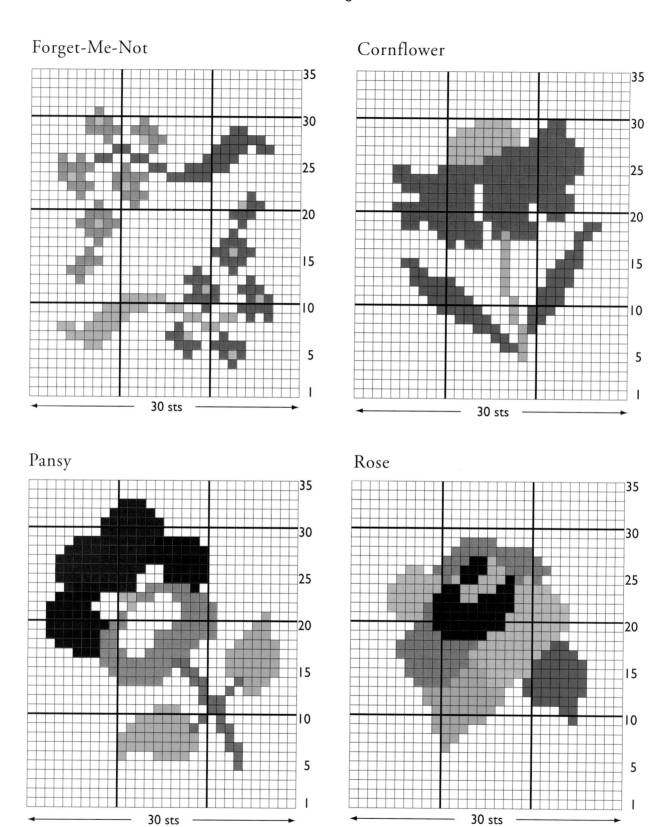

Cornflower

Pansy

Rose

Forget-Me-Not

Cornflower

Pansy

Rose

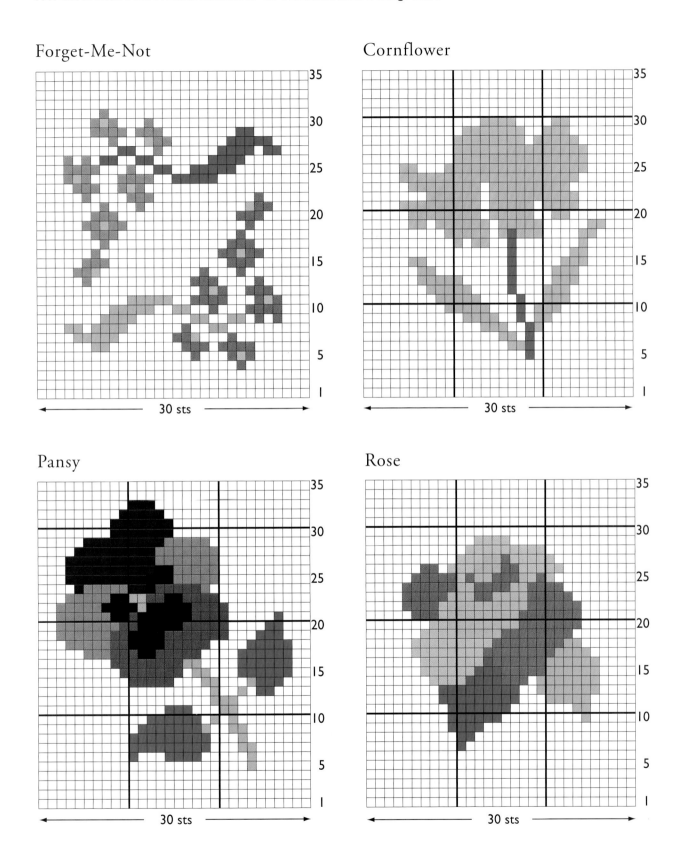

Techniques

TASSELS

Two types of tassels are used in this book.

Small Tassels

Cut a rectangle of cardboard as wide as the required length of the finished tassel. Wind the yarn around the card until the required thickness is reached. Break the yarn, thread through a sewing needle and pass the needle under all the loops. Do not remove the needle. Tie the end of the yarn firmly around the loops, remove the card and cut through the loops at the opposite end to the knot. Wind the end of the yarn around all the loops below the fold and fasten securely. Pass the needle through the top and use the end to sew in place. Trim the ends neatly.

Large Tassels

Make a tassel as directed under "Small Tassels"; then made a crochet head, using the yarn and crochet hook indicated in the pattern, as follows:

Base ring: 3 ch join with a sl st.

Round 1: 1 ch, 6 sc/dc into ring, sl st to 1st sc/dc.

Round 2: 1 ch, *1 sc/dc into next st, 2 sc/dc into foll st*. Rep from * to * (9 sc/dc), sl st to 1 sc/dc.

Round 3: 1 ch, *1 sc/dc into next st*. Rep from * to *, sl st to 1st sc/dc.

Round 4: work as for Round 2 (13 sc/dc).

Round 5 to Round 7: work as for Round 3.

Fasten off, leaving a long piece of yarn. Place tassel into top of tassel head. Thread yarn through a tapestry needle and wind round tassel a few times. Now sew tassel head onto tassel. Push needle up to top of tassel head and attach completed tassel to project (see photo on p. 50).

FRINGES

Two types of fringes are used in this book.

Simple Fringe

Cut lengths of yarn slightly more than twice the required length of the fringe. Fold the strands in half and draw the folded end through the edge of the knitted fabric using a crochet hook. Draw the loose ends of yarn through the loop and draw up firmly to form a knot.

Lattice Fringe

Make a Simple Fringe using 30" lengths of yarn. Then knot the fringe by tying 6 strands from one fringe to 6 strands of the next fringe across the row. Make 4 rows of knots.

Simple fringe

Lattice fringe

POMPONS

A pompon is used on the Rosehip Tam-o'-Shanter. Cut out two 2½"-diameter circles of thin cardboard. From the center of each circle, cut out a ¾" inner circle. Thread the yarn into a wool needle and, holding both cards together, wind it into the inner circle and back to the outside. Repeat this again and again, working round the outer circle evenly, until the inner circle is tightly filled. Joins should be made at the outer edge so that any unevenness can be trimmed off when the Pompon is complete. Once the center is filled, insert the tip of sharp scissors between the two cards and cut all around the outer edge. Push the cards apart so that you can tie a strand of yarn tightly and securely round all the strands through the center hole, leaving a tail on the strands. Cut the cards away. Trim off any uneven ends to obtain a smooth surface. The pompon can now be sewn in place with the strand tails.

BOBBLES

Bobbles are worked over several rows to give a raised effect and appear on the chart at the position to be worked.

Row 1: (K1 P1 K1) into next st, turn.

Row 2: K3, turn.

Row 3: P3, turn.

Row 4: K3, turn.

Row 5: P3 tog, then carry on with the chart.

The instructions are the same whenever a bobble occurs whether it is on a K row or a P row.

> **TIP:** Instead of working the bobbles as the knitting progresses, they can be made up separately and tied in place later before sewing in the loose ends. Bobbles made this way often turn out larger than those made as you go; so knit a row less in the middle of the bobble.

TWISTED RIB

A twisted rib gives a firmer rib than the usual K1 P1 rib. It is worked by knitting every K1 stitch through the back instead of the front of the loop.

TWISTED STITCHES

Twisted stitches are used in the Mock Cable Rib. The twist effect is produced by knitting into the second stitch on the left needle, stretching the stitch just made slightly, and then, without slipping off, knitting into the back of the first stitch. Both are then slipped off the left needle. The instructions are written as "twist 2 knitwise."

GARTER STITCH

Garter stitch is achieved by working every row as a knit row. Both sides of the work will be identical.

SEED STITCH/MOSS STITCH

The seed stitch, or moss stitch, is made up of alternate knit and purl stitches as in a K1 P1 rib; but rather than being kept in vertical lines, the stitches in seed stitch are worked at odds to those on the previous row. Thus a stitch that has been knitted on the first row will also be knitted on the second row.

SEAMS: MATTRESS STITCH

The mattress stitch is a most versatile stitch and should be used to join most of the pieces in this book. It provides a strong, invisible seam well-suited to side seams and seams that join two pieces of patterned knitting. This is because it is sewn with the right side facing, so you can match the pattern as you go. You will need a tapestry needle and some yarn.

1. Place the two seam edges side by side, right side up. Thread the needle and stitch through two stitchbars, one stitch in from the edge on one side.

2. Pick up the two stitchbars one stitch in on the other side.

3. Without pulling the stitches taut, pick up the next two stitchbars on the first side. Then pick up the next two stitchbars on the other side, and so on.

4. When the thread has been zigzagged across the two seam edges about five times, pull it taut—the seam will ease together. Continue until the seam is complete, as shown.

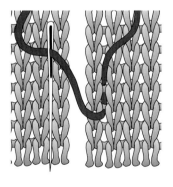
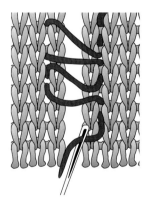

Resources

For details of the kits for knitting my designs or custom-knitted garments write to:

Sasha Kagan
The Studio
Y-Fron, Llawr-Y-Glyn, Caersws, Powys
SY17 5RJ UK

For information about my workshops and lectures go to:

www.sashakagan.com

For Rowan and Jaegar yarns in the UK and Europe write to:

Rowan Yarns
Green Lane Mill
Holmfirth, West Yorkshire
HD7 1RW, UK
www.rowanyarns.co.uk

For Rowan/Westminster Fibers in the United States write to:

Rowan/Westminster Fibers
5 Northern Blvd.
Amherst, NH 03031

For Jaegar yarns in the United States write to:

Knitting Fever, Inc.
P.O. Box 52
35 Debevoise Ave.
Roosevelt, NY 11575-0502

For Colinette yarn write to:

Banwy Workshops
Poole Rd.
Llanfair Caereinion, Powys
SY21 0SG UK
www.colinette.com

For Shetland yarn write to:

Jamieson & Smith
90 North Rd.
Lerwick, Shetland Isles
ZE1 0PQ UK

For Twilleys lurex in the UK write to:

Twilleys of Stamford
Roman Mill
Stamford Lines
PE9 1BG UK

For Twilleys lurex in the United States write to:

Beroco, Inc.
P.O. Box 367
14 Elmdale Rd.
Uxbridge, MA 01569